S0-BSX-011

G-4023

Common Hymnsense

Madeleine Forell Marshall

With a Foreword by John Ferguson

© 1995, GIA Publications, Inc.
7404 S. Mason Ave., Chicago, IL 60638
All rights reserved
Printed in the United States of America

Library of Congress Cataloging-in-Publication Data
Marshall, Madeleine Forell, 1946-
      Common hymnsense / Madeleine Forell Marshall; with a foreword by John Ferguson.
          p.   cm.
      ISBN 0-941050-69-6
      1. Hymns, English—History and criticism. 2. Hymns, American—History and criticism.
      I. Title.
      BV315.M37   1995
      264'.2'09—dc20   95-2774
                                                CIP

The following authors and publishers have generously given permission to use their texts:

A Mighty Fortress Is Our God
Text copyright © 1978 *Lutheran Book of worship*. Reprinted by permission of Augsburg Fortress

A Spendthrift Lover Is the Lord
Copyright and reproduced by permission of Oxford University Press. From *New Hymns for the Lectionary*

Christ Is Alive! Let Christians Sing
Copyright © 1975 by Hope Publishing Co., Carol Stream, IL 60188. All rights reserved. Used by permission

Come, Let Us Eat
St. 1–3: The Lutheran World Federation, P.O. Box 2100, 1211 Geneva 2, Switzerland.
St. 4: Text of stanza 4 copyright © 1972 *Contemporary Worship 4: Hymns for Baptism and Holy Communion.* Reprinted by permission of Augsburg Fortress

Earth and All Stars
Text copyright © 1968 Augsburg Publishing House. Reprinted by permission of Augsburg Fortress

Lift Ev'ry Voice and Sing
James Weldon Johnson, J. Rosamond Johnson. Used by permission of Edward B. Marks Music Company

Out of the Depths I Cry to You
Text copyright © 1978 *Lutheran Book of Worship.* Reprinted by permission of Augsburg Fortress

Rise, Shine, You People
Text copyright © 1974 Augsburg Publishing House. Reprinted by permission of Augsburg Fortress

This Touch of Love
Text copyright © 1987, Jaroslav J. Vajda. Used by permission

For Gary

If the Lord who inhabits the Praises of *Israel* shall refuse to smile upon this Attempt for the Reformation of Psalmody amongst the Churches, yet I humbly hope that his blessed Spirit will make these Composures useful to private Christians; and if they may but attain the Honour of being esteem'd pious Meditations, to assist the devout and the retir'd Soul in the Exercises of Love, Faith and Joy, 'twill be a valuable Compensation of my Labours; my Heart shall rejoice at the Notice of it, and my God shall receive the Glory.

Isaac Watts, 1709
Preface to *Hymns and Spiritual Songs*

Contents

Contents

Foreword

This is a fascinating book. It's thesis is deceptively simple: hymns are important and deserve our careful study. Yet in spite of the hundreds of books written about hymns, we have shied away from essential, fundamental questions about them. What do they mean? What do they say?

In attempting to answer these questions, the author encourages us to consider hymns as poetry, as literature that can be studied, literature whose meaning can be unpacked through rigorous examination. She demands that we focus on what hymns say and how they say it. She insists on precision and clarity, encouraging us to read hymns with care, with intelligence. She keeps asking the question, Does this hymn make sense?

In the process of leading us to a new level of critical thinking about hymnody, the rigorous tools of a literary historian are applied to a series of hymn texts. The study begins with the first English hymns (those of Watts and Wesley), adds examples of the traditions before Watts as they enter the English-speaking singers' repertoire through translation, and concludes with examples of contemporary hymnody. Thus we are given a brief overview of the historical development of hymnody through selected examples of congregational song.

This is a disturbing book. Comfortable notions are questioned. Some of our "favorites" are subjected to a level of scrutiny, an intellectual honesty, that yields surprising and often disturbing results. In the introduction, the author admits that "criticism—unlike hymns—tends to be summary, dogmatic, evaluative, biased, selective, and prone to academic pontification." But she goes on to make the essential point that "criticism, nevertheless, beats indifference." Some of her conclusions may upset us, and she encourages us to disagree with her, but we cannot deny the integrity of the process of examination which leads to her conclusions.

This is a devotional book. The author has not set out to write a book of brief devotions based upon a collection of hymns, yet she has done just that through her dedication to her discipline and application of her skills to an examination of hymn texts. One need not agree with the author's conclusions to discover with her that careful, critical study of the rich body of literature we call hymnody yields a fascinating variety of insights, both into our faith and into the evolution of hymnody itself. One need not agree with any specific criticism to discover the deepened understanding of the faith that careful reading of hymnody can bring. In this sense, the author gives the reader two gifts: a collection of devotional readings inspired by hymn texts and a set of tools for the critical reading of hymns—texts that can so strongly influence one's perception of what it means to be a Christian.

JOHN FERGUSON

St. Olaf College
Northfield, Minnesota

Acknowledgments

Many people have generously supported the writing and publication of *Common Hymnsense:* My husband and children have, for years, tolerated my unseemly behavior in church—my grimacing, muttering, notetaking, and ruffling around in hymnbooks—and exchanged ideas with me, over dinner, about particular texts. Mark Bangert, Paul Manz, and John Ferguson listened carefully to many of my early ideas and helped me along. Rebecca Slough tested an early draft of the project as a seminary textbook. My students at the Lutheran School of Theology at Chicago and participants in the Saint Olaf College Summer Music and Theology Program cheered me on and suggested hymns for the study. The meetings and publications of The Hymn Society in the United States and Canada provided important settings for the formulation of key ideas found in this book. Allan Mahnke, who first proposed the project and encouraged its progress, certainly deserves special credit. I am, finally, immensely grateful to Robert Batastini and GIA for making the publication of the book possible, to Neil Borgstrom, for his tireless copy-editing, and to the hymn writers who permitted the use of their texts in the following pages.

A Note on the Hymnals

The original texts of the hymns treated here have been compared with the texts as reproduced in the five following contemporary hymnals, listed in chronological order:

Lutheran Book of Worship, Augsburg Publishing House, 1978

The Hymnal 1982, "according to the use of The Episcopal Church," The Church Hymnal Corporation, 1982

Worship: A Hymnal and Service Book for Roman Catholics (Third edition), GIA Publications, Inc., 1986

The United Methodist Hymnal, The United Methodist Publishing House, 1989

The Presbyterian Hymnal, Westminster/John Knox Press, 1990

I normally abbreviate reference to these books by reporting what "Lutherans," "Episcopalians," "Catholics," "Methodists," or "Presbyterians" sing. Most readers will recognize that—however convenient—this misrepresents the complex status of any hymnal and the various roles these new hymnals play. Not all singers in a particular tradition use the most recent official hymnbook. *Worship* is, of course, in a category by itself, reflected in my alternating reference to "Catholics" and "GIA."

Sources of hymns are generally provided in the text. The reader interested in further bibliographic information is directed to any one of the many admirable "hymnal companions" or to John Julian's venerable *Dictionary of Hymnology.*

Reproducing the original version of eighteenth-century texts, I have preserved the original spelling and approximated the typography, including capital letters and italics. Literary historians have come to appreciate how these features suggest to the eye patterns of meaning and emphasis. I certainly do not mean to advocate the restoration of these interesting archaisms in contemporary hymnals!

Introduction

Hymns are important

Hymns matter to people in the pew: those people whose favorite hymns may irritate church musicians and pastors, those people who resist new hymnals with their well-intentioned omissions and changes in texts, those people who memorized hymns as children, sing hymns in the shower or in the car and recall hymn texts in mortal crises, perhaps in death.

Hymns matter to church musicians and pastors and editors of hymnals. Selecting appropriate hymns and arranging them to fit liturgical contexts and adjusting them to meet contemporary needs—these are important, time- and energy-consuming tasks. The time and energy suggest the importance of hymns to these professionals.

Quantitatively, a goodly portion of time in church is spent singing hymns—even a goodlier portion if we count, as we should, liturgical hymns and psalms and choral anthems and hymn preludes played on the organ. Certainly the bulk of our worship books is made up of hymns.

Despite such evidence that hymns are important, most people—the ordinary folk in the pew and the professionals who shape and direct their song—have only a vague idea of what hymns are and how they work. We all know hymns are songs, sometimes somehow "fun," and that they have something to do with praising God. But that's about it. Certain lines and pictures may stand out or stick in our minds, but the larger sense of how hymns function eludes us.

Evidence nevertheless abounds of the felt need to know more about hymns. Every new hymnal has its "companion," a compendium of biographical and historical information about hymn writers and composers and the changes in hymn texts. Hundreds of books have been written about hymns. Pastors often talk about hymns and hymn writers in sermons and meditations. We've perhaps heard rumors of controversy raging about "O" versus "Oh" and "I" versus "We" hymns.

Despite all this interest and attention, the basic issues of definition and function are rarely touched. What exactly do hymns do? How do they work? Exactly what do they mean? Why are they so important? These questions, asked of particular texts and of hymns in general, deserve our attention.

Hymns are poems

If we are to ask these questions, we have to confront the central, fascinating trouble with hymns: they are poems. Publishers have tried to avoid dealing with hymns as poetry by printing them to follow lines of music in our hymnals, a custom that effectively disguises them. Pious specialists in hymnody have helped us avoid reading hymns as poems by declaring that hymns are *more* than poems (suggesting, perhaps, that poetry is frivolous). Hymn scholars have encouraged us to see hymn study as the accumulation of facts and details about hymn writers and texts—rather than the careful reading of poems. This business of treating hymns as poems is indeed a challenge.

We are very confused about poetry. On the one hand it matters profoundly and is as natural as breathing: Our greeting cards and popular songs suggest that we turn to poetry when we have important messages to send and crises to cope with. We have all written poetry, perhaps complete poems, perhaps a line or idea here or there. In school we were encouraged to "express our feelings" in lines of verse. Perhaps some of our poems made their way into literary magazines. Perhaps we had to memorize a few dozen lines of Longfellow or Frost or Sandburg. Poems are sprinkled through popular magazines—and less popular magazines, too.

On the other hand, poems make us anxious. In school most of us never quite got the point. They told us poetry was important and there were pretty images—but it all seemed a little beyond our depth. Rhymes we could identify and similes announced themselves with *as* or *like*. Metaphors and imagery and rhetorical devices were tougher. And what did these things have to do with the profound *feelings* poetry was supposed to be about?

Although I have now taught poetry for more than twenty years, I can easily think my way back into the frustration of studying poetry: the explanations that didn't connect with the words on the page, the seeming nonsense of those words, the apparent need for volumes of background information, the sense of never quite having "got" it. Why would anyone want to burden our much-loved hymnody with the cruel weight of poetry?

Complicating the picture even further, we have all heard that poetry is a state of mind, a song of the soul, a cry from the heart, or some such non-sense. Our private response has been encouraged in the classroom while insistence on intelligible, sharable meaning has been frustrated. How can reading hymns as poems help us understand them if poetry is, by defini-tion, highly personal and basically beyond common understanding?

The answer is that hymns are a particularly transparent kind of poetry, a kind of poetry that depends for its usefulness and its success on its acces-sibility to common understanding. That's not to say it's mindlessly simple or just like prose. Hymns, as poetry, work within strict formal constraints—but these are familiar patterns of regular tunes, much simpler than sonnets. Hymns, as poetry, make use of networks of image and meaning—but these networks are familiar from the Bible and from Sunday school and sermons and from everyday experience. Hymns, as poetry, concentrate meaning, avoid filler words and decoration. They have to be densely meaningful if we are to sing them over and over, to memorize them, if they are to mean new things to us at different stages of life, in different circumstances. Prose can't bear that kind of strain.

One more word about poetry and emotion, for now: States of mind, songs of the soul, and cries of the heart—so often associated with poetry—these are presumably inarticulate, nonverbal, raw emotion.

Poetry, in contrast, is an art form. Its material is words, with all their associations, carefully chosen and arranged on the page. Poetry asks us to focus sharply on just what it's saying and how. Poetry won't tolerate vagueness and imprecision. Poetry is demanding.

Congregational songs of praise?

The simplest-seeming definition of the sort of hymns we sing in church is probably as "congregational songs of praise." Although it seems obvious that hymns are songs, meant for congregational singing, let's be careful: thousands of hymns have been written and printed and never set or sung to music. Because they were meant for congregational singing, they are hymns nevertheless. Similarly, hymns we recall in the car or the shower remain hymns outside the context of collective worship. Their meaning may be slightly different, their function more personal, but they remain hymns. Generally, however, congregational singing is normative, assumed by the hymn writer and understood by the reader.

As congregational songs, hymns are strictly limited in form and content and attitude. These limitations provide a very real set of creative challenges. The first hymns in English had to fit the tunes people knew, the three simple patterns of the metrical psalms. While we have countless tunes today, the patterns, perhaps coded in the back of your hymnal, are still relatively few. Rhyme is standard, even in the late twentieth century; it goes with the hymn territory. While the requirements of song are fierce, the requirements of *congregational* song are even fiercer. Hymns are no place to express private visions or fears, even in a day of the alienated and isolated creative sensibility. The attitudes and responses must be sanctioned, permitted, approved for common use. If they cannot be shared, the hymn, however touching as a poetic expression, fails as congregational song.

So what are hymns about? Are they "songs of praise"? I think not. Let me suggest that praise—like the states of mind, the songs of the soul, and the cries of the heart mentioned above—is not something that words can express. Hymns are not expressions of praise but something else entirely. They urge us to praise, inspire us to praise, tell us why we should, how we

4

should, when we should praise God. They are not, in themselves, praise but rather instruction in praise. (This conclusion is not based on some erudite theological understanding but on the careful survey of thousands of hymns. Certainly one benefit of the careful reading of our hymns should be such startling ideas.)

Our quintessential "song of praise" is probably Thomas Ken's "Praise God, from Whom All Blessings Flow," familiar from church picnics. As we sing it, we move, under Bishop Ken's careful guidance, from the simplest, most familiar and lowly acknowledgment of God as source of all good things, to an appreciation of our status as creatures, to a view of ourselves in a larger, transcendent frame, a context that allows us to invoke the Trinity. Our eyes rise from the blessings to God:

> Praise God, from whom all blessings flow;
> Praise him, all creatures here below;
> Praise him above, ye heav'nly host;
> Praise Father, Son, and Holy Ghost.

Lutheran Book of Worship, #564

In the first line we, the singers, tell each other to, indeed, praise God, identified as the source of all blessings. This idea of God as source is rich and suggestive: that which "flows" proceeds naturally and inevitably, like water down a hill. A "flow," as opposed to a trickle, is generous and constant. Material that "flows" is visible at our feet.

The second line extends our command to all created beings. Following Bishop Ken's script, we remind ourselves that we are one kind of creature, one of many. We recall the fullness of creation that surrounds us as well as our own creation, good reasons for praise. The established rising movement next takes us to the heavenly host, the ranks of angels brought into the song in the third line. We are ready to raise our sights above the familiar blessings and the known creation, to see praise as an immortal and eternal activity. This, finally, is the understanding that permits us to praise the mystery of the Trinity.

It's a fine table grace if we understand how it works, how we are led, through the poetry, from the food to consider the work of creation, to our sanctification, to the glory of God. We are told who is to praise and why; we are led carefully from tangible goods to intangible glories; we are "uplifted" and prepared for praise that is, presumably, inexpressible.

In fact, many hymns are not particularly concerned with praise at all. They may tell stories or paint pictures or dramatize events. Their purpose is to shape our understanding of our faith, to teach us Christian attitudes, and to drill us in proper response. They may remind us that our God is like a mighty fortress, a strong ally, which we often forget. They describe the drama of the Christian life, the cruel oppressors, the evil foe, the hordes of devils. Singing these memorable formulations, we learn how we should feel. Hymns are, above all, educational, written to lead us in the paths of righteousness, of right attitudes, and of Christian understanding. Hymns are efforts at spiritual formation, at guided response. Certainly, if this is so, we must read them very carefully.

Selecting texts for study

The historical development of the congregational hymn is a necessary part of any study of its design and function. Hymns are, even more than other kinds of literature, written within a tradition, following an established pattern. Hymns are written to meet certain specific needs and certain expectations. They have to fit into worship, to be commonly understandable, to be useful to the people who sing them. They have had to fit available music, to rhyme, to speak to singers' experience. Hymn writers assimilate the models of their predecessors and follow them—or take exception to them. They always, unavoidably, write with reference to them.

The most obvious approach to the study of congregational hymnody is to examine hymns in chronological order. This calls for a tracing of psalms and other biblical prototypes, early Greek and Latin hymnody, medieval song, Reformation song, Pietist and other seventeenth-century hymns and psalms. Only then would we turn to hymns written in English, the work of Isaac Watts and Charles Wesley, followed by nineteenth-century

Scandinavian and American work. Most hymn history follows this progression and includes vast numbers of texts from many traditions. Such histories are widely available and the standard fare of hymnal companions.

This study follows a different route, tracing the development of the hymn in English for English-speaking singers. This approach is based on the observation that, while our standard theological traditions may be Germanic or Scandinavian, our hymns are poems in English, with an English history. Most of us know the tradition before Watts only through the medium of English translation, a process that effectively transforms texts into items of the English tradition. We know Latin hymnody and the great German hymns of the Reformation and of Pietism as they were reworked by Victorian poets, recasting the texts to meet the expectations of singers brought up on Watts and Wesley and Reginald Heber.

Accordingly, we shall begin with Watts, not because he was the first person ever to write hymns but because he was the first to write congregational hymns widely sung in English and his work provided a model for English-language hymns to follow. Certainly Watts was an accomplished scholar who knew the work of his predecessors, Hebrew, Greek, Latin, and (as I argue elsewhere) German. He was a remarkably influential preacher and educator, whose work was widely read in England and America, and an important churchman for whom the introduction of hymns into worship represented a real opportunity for congregational renewal. Finally, he was a fine poet, who teaches us, just as he taught his singers almost three hundred years earlier, to read hymns with careful attention.

We test the reading skills we learn from Watts as we apply them to selected work of Charles Wesley. Some of Wesley's hymns are sprawling, undisciplined productions; others are finely crafted, succinct, and powerful texts. The differences are instructive. The Olney hymns of John Newton and William Cowper, both their similarities to and differences from Watts and Wesley, further refine our critical discrimination and our understanding of what hymns were in the eighteenth century.

Turning to the nineteenth century, we compare and contrast the work of the two most prominent Anglican hymn writers, Bishop Reginald Heber and John Mason Neale. The comparison allows us to observe the new poeticization of hymnody, introduced by Heber, and the assimilation of ancient

Greek and Latin texts, as adapted by Neale. These works are then compared to a sampling of the popular hymnody of Ray Palmer, Joseph Gilmore, Elizabeth Clephane, and Frances Havergal. Because Catherine Winkworth, a nineteenth-century poet, remains the foremost English translator of German hymnody, German hymns are treated in this nineteenth-century context.

Any "modern" selection is always the most tentative, the least objective. Indeed, selection of modern texts demonstrates how any selection, whether for a hymn collection or for a critical study, becomes a kind of canonization. We have not tried any harder here to be comprehensive than in earlier sections. Twentieth-century hymns are simply grouped in three categories: third-world and liberation hymns, experimental hymnody, and modern hymns that follow more traditional understanding. The first category is political; the second and third are formal.

Within this historical framework, we shall work with *familiar* hymns, texts in common use, so familiar that we rarely stop to consider what they mean or how they work. This standard of familiarity is fairly subjective. I haven't gone to statistical tables or studies of hymn use but, rather, selected texts from the *Lutheran Book of Worship* that I (as a Lutheran) have sung since early childhood, arranging them to fit the historical curve of the English hymn. Many more great hymns are left out than I have included— hymns in the *Lutheran Book of Worship* as well as hymns lost in time. I only hope that the "reading" modeled in these pages will be useful to others as they look at the texts omitted here.

The hymns we treat here were chosen to encourage a renewed interest in reading hymn texts intelligently. (Even the historical progression serves that goal.) The main argument of this little book, which the texts support, is so simple it hardly deserves the name. It maintains that hymns, as they are important, can and should make clear, fine sense to anybody who reads or sings them. It further demonstrates that hymns—for one reason or another—often don't make sense, and that this is deplorable. These hymns have worked well in workshops and classes I have taught. Students, indeed, first brought several of the texts to my attention. While the sequence is not meant to support any ambitious literary or theological thesis, it naturally expresses my own taste and bias, upbringing, and experience. (While I might have pretended otherwise, such bias is unavoidable and such pretense would be irresponsible.)

Lest I appear disingenuous, let me be even more precise: My main argument, the rightful intelligibility of congregational hymnody, both its importance and its frequent failure, should be distinguished from subordinate arguments that emerge in passing. I shall, in my readings of certain texts, argue for the use of inclusive language, delight in texts packed with multiple meaning, debunk the traditional distinction between "I" hymns and "We" hymns, prefer Watts to Wesley and Neale to Heber and Troeger to Wren, and prophesy about the dangers of hymnological tourism passing for cross-cultural understanding. While I hope these subordinate arguments are convincing, what matters most is the scrutiny of meaning, the exact tracking of what's going on in the texts. This cause, not the other convictions, has determined the selection of texts.

The texts themselves

Our focus in the following chapters will be on the texts of the hymns, the words on the page, with almost no reference to the lives and times of the hymn writers. The biographies of hymn writers are readily available in hymnal companions and other reference works. Indeed, hymnologists have tended to indulge very heavily in biographical criticism, as though the lives and piety of the writers somehow explained the texts. The connection between life and text is, however, rarely made by the hymnologists, and the biographies generally fail to help us understand the hymns.

The tendency to celebrate the lives of hymn writers while ignoring the design and language of their texts suggests a critical understanding of hymns as *expressions* of the personalities of their authors, an understanding of hymns with which I take issue. While certain hymns (many hymns of Charles Wesley are examples) proceed from personal experience, the hymn works as a hymn only to the extent that the personal is generalized, to the extent that it becomes common property, common experience. The piety of a hymn is certified correct, appropriate, recommended piety, not the expression of the attitudes and secret thoughts of a particularly pious person. If this is so, then the lives of the hymn writers, although admittedly sometimes fascinating, are of little consequence to the singer or student of hymns. While this may seem like a cruelly extreme position, it effectively balances the common indulgence in a hagiography of hymn writers, who are always described as wonderful, faithful, sensitive, holy men and women who have suffered.

Turning to the texts, we immediately face the issues of alteration and adaptation. It is ironic that while the excellence of great hymn writers has been praised to the skies, the original integrity of their poetry has never been much respected. The texts we shall study have all been altered—some well, some badly, some heavily, some only slightly. Some hymns are cut to pieces and pasted back together. Many stanzas are missing. Many expressions are changed. How ought we to react to alteration?

I think that we first should acknowledge that hymns are living texts, not historical artifacts. They are only valuable to the extent that they work for modern singers. Language changes over time. The understanding of the human condition changes over time. Varieties of religious experience familiar in one era are alien to another. Living texts must be adapted or discarded. Hymn texts are not Scripture—but if they were, we note how even Scripture is regularly retranslated, which means altered and adapted, to make sense to each era.

The best example is the moving bowels of God. According to standard old psychology, pity was felt in the "bowels." In eighteenth-century hymns God's bowels move with compassion. Obviously, this won't fly in a modern congregation and either the text must be cut or altered or discarded. A second example is the image of humanity as depraved and wormlike. While our ancestors were unperturbed, we can only tolerate so many singing worms in our hymns. Language that is perhaps less misleading but still archaic to the point of unintelligibility must be edited. If hymns make no sense, we discourage attentive singing and might as well quit.

Under the pressure of feminist criticism, our language has changed radically in the last twenty years. We may approve or disapprove of the change, but it must be acknowledged. Clever students simply think "man" refers to the male sex, even in old poetry. Their professors have to explain the old usage the way they explain the vocabulary of Chaucer. Students learn to write inclusive English, and they read texts alert to gender differences that I may easily miss. Journalists and public speakers use inclusive English. Advertisers and scriptwriters use inclusive English. These pages are written using inclusive English. Normative American English has simply changed.

If we agree that hymns must make sense to modern singers and we acknowledge that the language has changed, we must allow our hymns to be adapted to the modern idiom. Having said this, let me go on to say that this must be done with extreme care and, further, that I don't think proper care has been exercised. Caught up in a rush of inclusive enthusiasm, editors have taken terrible liberties, confusing the images, compromising precision, cutting away healthy tissue. They have often failed to analyze exactly what the hymn is doing, its images, the progression of its ideas, the devotional process behind the design. This failure to consider what is at stake has undermined many hymns.

I have reproduced in their entirety the original texts of most of the older hymns we shall treat. I have further noted the particularly significant alterations found in the series of major contemporary hymnals beginning with the *Lutheran Book of Worship*. This is no malicious attack on these editors but rather an essential part of my argument, evidence that hymns are not read carefully—by pastors, musicians, singers, or editors—and they should be. We should hold these texts accountable. They must make rich, good sense.

Finally, I have tried hard to avoid summary evaluations of hymns—the old Siskel and Ebert "thumbs up, thumbs down." I have tried to avoid dogmatic conclusions. Neither evaluation nor conclusion is in keeping with our general goal of close examination. Neither bashing nor praising texts serves that end. I realize that I have failed. Judgments—inevitably biased—are apparent in the selection of hymn texts and the shaping of each chapter. My own taste and expectations often intrude. Although the idea has been to model reading of hymns, one after another, I have indulged in little digressions and an occasional manifesto. I have likewise tried to avoid the excesses of academic prose, but realize that often the temptation has overwhelmed me. I fear that criticism—unlike hymns—tends to be summary, dogmatic, evaluative, biased, selective, and prone to academic pontification. Criticism, nevertheless, beats indifference.

"Reading" hymns

Hymns may usefully be approached from many directions. Their music and its theoretical, practical, and historical relationship to hymn texts is a very interesting and important approach. The relationship of hymns to the Christian cultures that produced them and to our own cultural experience suggests fascinating material for study. The biblical origins of hymns, their theological nuances, their liturgical contexts and homiletical connections—all are exciting fields for research. Favorite hymns take on meanings and associations for the individuals and communities who sing them, a fine subject for psychological-anthropological investigation. Hymns are subtly related to contemporary art, drama, architecture, choral music, even current events.

Then there are the practical studies. The process of compiling hymnals is a fascinating subject, including the selection and editing of texts and their presentation. The introduction of new hymns and hymnals, issues of congregational taste, proper accompaniment, who chooses Sunday's hymns—all are lively subjects.

All of these exciting possibilities seem, however, contingent on the precise tracking of meaning of the words of a hymn text on the page. We need to determine just what is happening with the words if we are successfully to relate the words to church history, theology, music, liturgical experience, or cultural values and artifacts. Exact reading is to hymnology as basic laboratory or field research is to physics or biology. It's foundational, logically precedent.

Moreover, we note how all of these interesting hymnological endeavors seem to demand uncommon sorts of expertise, special knowledge in academic disciplines—music, history, art, theology, social science, educational theory. Of course there's nothing wrong with such expertise. We value it. The men and women who select and sing congregational hymns, however, songs *by definition* of the people, should not need to resort to expert information. They may want to, but they shouldn't have to.

The active reading of hymns we intend to practice here is a different order of study, demanding no special equipment or tools except basic familiarity with English and a dictionary. The "study" simply asks careful attention to the words on the page, the deployment of skills we all use when we examine other important texts—special offers or contracts or love letters. The childlike appearance of many of the questions we ask of the texts in the following pages suggests that, as Watts would have it, everybody is capable of hymn reading:

1. Who is speaking? to whom? This is the question of address. The answers establish the situation of the hymn. Are "we" angels or sinners or ordinary people in the pew? Who are "they"? Are they saints or disciples or devils in hell? Is "you" God or Jesus or the worldly or the righteous? Who are the players here?

2. What is going on? This is the question of action. Am "I" pleading for mercy, expressing desperation, describing a vision, recalling conversion?

3. What happens first, next, last? How does the hymn progress from stanza to stanza? What is happening in the refrain? How are the events ordered?

4. What is the upshot or resolution? Where have we gone in the hymn? from despair to hope? puzzlement to confidence? blurred view to clear vision? Why do we sing it?

5. What do the words mean and why were they chosen? What's a herald angel? an oblation?

Children like puns and we can learn from their pleasure to appreciate *reign* as *rain* and *sun* as *son*. We can also ask, quite firmly, what's being compared to what when "sorrow and blood flow mingled down" the body of Christ. As we find the answers to such perfectly reasonable questions, we learn to trust hymn texts, to let them work on us. (Why does Neale have the faithful "raise the strain"?) If we ask the questions and read carefully, we may expect hymns, as songs of the people, to yield up their answers.

I: The Psalter Hymns of Isaac Watts

Joy to the World

"Joy to the World," by Isaac Watts (1674–1748), is a good place to begin. We all know the hymn by heart and love it dearly. But what does it mean and how does it work on us and how much of our affection is really for the familiar cheerful music? In fact, it's a rich and wonderful poem that can support the weight of our inquiry. We shall begin with the text as poem, as it was originally printed, and proceed to take it apart, "unpacking" it phrase by phrase.

The Messiah's Coming and Kingdom

1. Joy to the World; the Lord is come;
   Let Earth receive her King

> Let every Heart prepare him Room,
> And Heaven and Nature sing.

> 2. Joy to the Earth, The Saviour reigns;
> Let Men their Songs employ;
> While Fields & Floods, Rocks, Hills & Plains
> Repeat the sounding Joy.

> 3. No more let Sins and Sorrows grow,
> Nor Thorns infest the Ground:
> He comes to make his Blessings flow
> Far as the Curse is found.

> 4. He rules the World with Truth and Grace,
> And makes the Nations prove
> The Glories of his Righteousness,
> And Wonders of his Love.

The first phrase, although so familiar and so seemingly simple, is actually a little puzzle. "Joy to the World," originally closed with a semicolon, should be a complete grammatical unit, but there's no verb. We properly ask, What joy? Why this joy? and What does "joy to the world" mean? The hymn sets out to answer just those questions. Once we understand, we return to the initial phrase, revised at the start of the second stanza, and understand it as benediction, a formula and a grammatical pattern familiar from Gospel blessings as in "Grace and peace to you."

Meanwhile, we sing "the Lord is Come"—not the more expected "has come," which would suggest achievement, but the active, present arrival of the Lord. As this second half of the first line carefully builds a pattern of associations with the first half, the reason for *is* rather than *has* grows even clearer:

$$
\begin{array}{ccc}
\text{JOY} & .. & \text{WORLD} \\
: & \text{to/is} & : \\
\text{LORD} & .. & \text{COME}
\end{array}
$$

The second phrase is in apposition to the first, amplifying and explaining it: the Lord *is* Joy, the Coming *is to* the World, Joy *is* come, the Messiah *is* the Lord of the World. The substance of the benediction, the cause for joy, is the coming of the Lord. Juxtaposed, the two simple phrases convey a great deal more than the awkward paraphrase: Let the world rejoice because the Lord has come. In such a paraphrase, the benediction, the identification of Lord and Joy, and the presentness of the coming are all lost.

Moving on to the second line, we rightly ask why the change from *World* ("Joy to the World") to *Earth* ("Let Earth receive . . ."). *World* had seemed a simple enough idea until Watts replaced it with *Earth*. (He will return to *World* at the beginning of the last stanza.) In fact, we do well to consider the differences between these synonyms, which aren't really interchangeable. Either may refer to our planet and its inhabitants; and worldly and earthly affairs are both contrasted to heavenly concerns. However, *world* is a broader and more metaphorical concept. We speak, for example, of "the academic world" or "the business world" or "the animal world," of "the new world," and of "worldviews." In none of these expressions can we replace *world* with *earth*. *Earth* is always tangible, visible, underfoot. Our bodies are formed of earth and return to earth.

The Earth, not the World, is, in basic, universal human mythology, powerfully female, the source and end of life. Caves and wombs, graves and tombs, seeds in the earth—it's a rich complex, approachable through classical mythology (where Persephone, daughter of the fertility goddess Demeter, marries Hades and goes to live in the dark underground for six months of the year), through countless poems, through Freudian and Jungian psychology, or through common experience of pregnancy and burial.

This is the Earth which is to receive *her* King. This reception suggests the mythological marriage of Earth and Sky (the God of Heaven) which was creation. We have moved from the fairly abstract political idea of the first line, "the Lord of the World," to a much more suggestive and vastly more interesting understanding of creation.

This is *not* to say that Watts was a Goddess enthusiast. It *is* to say that fine poetry explaining the transformation of creation accomplished by the Incarnation turns naturally toward sexual imagery, rooted in earth with its powerful female associations. Ironically, the Lutherans have altered the hymn so that "earth receives its King," striking the powerful—and arguably powerfully feminist—female personification of Earth. As the Episcopalians, Catholics, Methodists, and Presbyterians retain the female Earth, they seem to acknowledge her metaphorical power.

Line 3 demonstrates a marvelous sort of zoom-lens poetic technique (familiar from seventeenth-century metaphysical poetry). We have, with the Earth and her King, been imagining supersize female and male mythological figures, engaged in cosmic creation. Suddenly we zoom in to the individual human heart, which is asked to prepare its own room for the Lord. There's bridal imagery here, by the conventions of which each believer is understood as mystically married to the Lord. In divine love poetry, modeled on the Song of Songs, the Spouse invites the Bridegroom into her mother's house, her room. This is a rich and evocative and controversial tradition. The call for "room" naturally and delicately reminds us of another domestic scene as well: the father and the mother, pregnant with new creation, for whom there was no room in the inn.

By the time we come to line 4 a whole network of strong and immediate associations has been strung up, ranging from creation mythology to divine love imagery to Mary and Joseph. The song of Heaven and Nature in line 4 is in fact a fine duet, a marriage song, explaining the meaning of Christmas in terms we can appreciate.

The first line of the second stanza repeats the construction of the first line, but with subtle differences. The Earth, with all its basic female fertility associations of soil and clay and planting and procreation and burial, is to rejoice. (See Psalm 98:4.) We understand the basic idea because of our experience of the first stanza: the working of salvation on earth is no subtle, abstract occurence. The joy is because the *Saviour* (rather than the Lord) *reigns*. We normally separate out the saving (horizontal) from the ruling (vertical) attributes of Christ. Watts refuses this separation—the whole point of the "Messiah's Coming" of the title, the whole point of the Incarnation, it seems, is that the one who *reigns* is saving creation. (We may well marvel that those same compilers of the Episcopal, Catholic, Methodist, and Presbyterian hymnals who respected the female Earth all opted to alter Watts's original "Joy to the Earth," changing it to repeat "Joy to the World!" Only the Lutherans move, with Watts, from one joy to the next.)

We wouldn't be doing our job if we failed to point out that, to our ears, *reigns* is the same word as *rains*. Just as the rain of water from the sky makes new life possible on earth, so the reign of the Savior transforms the earth. Part of the network of meaning and association, this is no idle pun.

Turning to the second line, the last word, however familiar the hymn, gives us pause. When Watts, the "Father of English Hymnody," writes about singing, we do well to pay close attention. What does it mean to "employ" songs? We may "sing" them or "write" them or "play" them—and Watts could have handled any of these rhymes with perfect finesse. He chose, however, to command people to "employ" their songs. Come to think of it (and look it up), it's a rich and subtle word. *Employ* means "make use of" as in the expression "to employ a pen for sketching." By implication, our songs are *tools we use. Employ* also carries an archaic sense of "dispatching with a commission." Our songs are also *dispatches we send.* Most commonly, *employ* means to "engage the services of" and we *engage the services of* song in our hymnody. Each of these meanings tells us something about how songs *work. Employ* also anticipates important ideas of the next stanza. "Employment" is labor, the curse of Adam after the Fall.

The natural world of the following line, the world of "Fields & Floods, Rocks, Hills & Plains," is carefully described. The Fields are where, since the Fall, we labor, employed planting and harvesting. Fields thus tie into the network of fertility images, of growing things, the nature that sings in duet with heaven. Fields also recall the shepherds, who kept their sheep in the fields and returned from Bethlehem to the fields, glorifying God. Fields may remind us, finally, of the Parable of the Sower and the planting of the Gospel. Floods recall the reign/rain pun of the first line, the water of fertility, as well as God moving on the waters. Noah's flood, the flood as daily high tide, flood as elemental water—these are all implied in the flood of stanza 2. Rocks and Hills recall the rocky ground, the tomb, the hills to which I lift up mine eyes. The Plains invoke the Messianic promise of Isaiah, "the crooked made straight and the rough places, plain." All of nature, substantial geological nature, repeats the song, celebrating the coming, the Kingdom, the redemption of the natural world.

The idea of nature echoing human song is a poetic commonplace, especially familiar from lyric poetry. The shepherd sighs and the wind echoes his sadness; the laughing brook, the moaning pines, the cloudy skies all reflect the poetic moods of human beings. (This is sometimes called the "pathetic fallacy.") In the last line of the second stanza this is happening, but with a very significant difference. All of nature (not just the wind) echoes human joy (not just the mood of a particular shepherd), not from poetic convention but because all of nature is, like all humanity, transformed by the Incarnation.

Finally, we may ask why nature repeats the "sounding" joy? Turning again to the dictionary, we note that *sounding (sound)* means many things: (1) That which is "sound" is healthy, wholesome (as in "sound in body and mind"), free from structural weakness (as in "sound construction"). By implication, the Joy, come to the world, is "sounding"—making us whole and healthy, restoring us to strength. (2) An archaic meaning of *sound* as "rumor or tidings" is also helpful—the joyful good news is "sounding" through the world. (3) *Sound* may further signify a "noise without meaning." Perhaps our joy—like our praises, our cries of the heart and secret thoughts and desires—is essentially incapable of articulation, hence "sounding." (4) *Sound* may, more commonly, mean to "make a noise," to "voice" or "put into words," and "to proclaim." All of these fit with the Joy we are called to sing and all creation to repeat. (5) Last, and most interesting, we note the idea of *sounding* as fathoming or measuring the depth of something. Indeed, the Joy that reaches from heaven to the depths of the earth "sounds" all creation.

In stanza 3 we find ourselves in a garden, the garden of nature, where the children of Adam and Eve have been employed, according to the Curse of the last line of the stanza, since the Fall. The imagery of Earth has been pointing us in this direction since line 2 of the first stanza. The Ground that is infested with thorns (line 2) is the Earth who receives her King, whose righteousness makes us "sound" in joy. We may regret the replacement of plural *Sins* and *Sorrows* with singular *sin* and *sorrow* in the Lutheran hymnal: the singular sin and sorrow undermine the important association with plural *thorns,* disconnecting the metaphor. (The Episcopalians, Methodists, and Presbyterians have kept the plurals, while the GIA text has compromised on singular sin and plural sorrows.) In the original, the quantity of sins and sorrows, as well as their nastiness, their quality, make them thorn-like. This gardening metaphor is continued in the idea of Blessings that flow (line 3). The blessings that flow in a garden are restorative rain waters from heaven, making new life possible. This healthful, life-giving water contrasts with the water of the Flood, perhaps recalling the water of baptism, drowning sins and sorrows, canceling the curse. (The Flood, in contrast, drowned life in judgment.)

Viewed within this frame, details of the imagery stand out sharply: Sins and Sorrows, basically abstract ideas, become as real and familiar as weeds in a garden. (This is a familiar idea, as in Hamlet's first soliloquy : "Fie on't, ah fie! 'tis an unweeded garden / That grows to seed, things rank and gross in nature / Possess it merely" [I, ii].) These weeds are not *natural* in the philosophical sense, but a corruption of nature—hence an infestation, like fleas or cockroaches. Choosing *thorns* rather than *weeds* to stand for sins and sorrows, Watts recalls the crown of thorns, worn by the Savior King whom the Earth is to receive—thorny emblems of the Fall and of the transformation it wrought in the order of nature. The Curse, according to Genesis, was of labor (sweaty employment) and suffering in childbirth: the first aspect of the curse is removed when we are employed in song and when the weeds stop growing; the removal of the sorrows of procreation is entailed in the new, fertile marriage of heaven and nature.

Watts has, in his three stanzas, directed us through a detailed examination of what this "Joy to the World" means, ranging over a vast amount of common human experience and theological interpretation. Now we can proceed really to understand "The Messiah's Coming and Kingdom" in the final stanza. We understand the "World" he rules in knowable terms of the earth and of the human experience, since Eden, of corruption. To *rule* is to govern but also to measure, recalling the measuring sense of *sounding* and also the geometric idea of *righteousness*. The acknowledgment by the nations of the Lord's rule, once we comprehend its extent, is inevitable and appropriate.

So the Lord "*Makes* the Nations *prove*" his achievement: "Made" to see, they have no choice. Their experience demonstrates the truth of ("proves") his righteousness and love. That "righteousness" is the right-making of all things, its restoration in the Kingdom, itemized in the forego-ing stanzas. The "Wonders of his Love" have been catalogued, from the cosmic marriage of the incarnation to nature's redemption on Calvary: the blessings flow. The nations have no choice, the Lord *is* come.

Treating "The Messiah's Coming and Kingdom" as a text, we have intentionally deferred any talk of its relationship to the psalm it "imitates" or to its customary music. When we remember that the singers for whom Watts wrote knew the metrical psalms and their tunes by heart, some com-mentary seems necessary. Certainly it took both nerve and authority on Watts's part to presume to imitate familiar biblical poetry. Turning to Psalm 98, we recognize the joy, the new song, the witness of the ends of the earth (1–3); the joyful noise of the earth before the king (4–6); the animated noise of sea, floods, and hills before the Lord, who "will judge the world with righteousness, and the people with equity" (7–9). Watts has reworked these familiar components in the Gospel framework, assimilating the psalm to Christian worship. The original singers of Watts's hymn must have sung it with reference to Psalm 98, as a commentary and explanation of the joyful noise of the earth. This juxtaposition added a further layer of meaning.

The original singers knew nothing of our tune, the familiar nineteenth-century ANTIOCH, which all five of our hymnals attribute to Handel. Their ignorance may have been something of an advantage. When we have examined the text closely, it becomes apparent that the tune—however exciting—distorts the text. The multiple repetitions of the last line, demanded by the tune, are not quite right. They throw each stanza out of balance and encourage a sort of incantatory, mindless enthusiasm, spoiling the careful progression of ideas. One indication that this is a distortion is the absence of terminal punctuation at the end of each third line, before the line highlighted by repetition. "And Heaven and Nature sing," for example, is no longer really continuous with the commands to earth and every heart in the lines before. It takes on a life of its own, not quite coher-ent. Just so, "Repeat the sounding Joy," repeated over and again, loses its proper meaning as we the singers, rather than all of nature, do the repeat-ing. "Far as the Curse is found," severed from the flood of blessings, makes little sense, while, finally, the "Glories of his Righteousness" slink into the background of the repeated "Wonders of his Love," another distortion.

This is, we must admit, hymnological heresy: First we stripped the text of its tune, then criticized the beloved tune as inappropriate. But try this text with a tune from the psalters Watts and his parishioners knew. When we count the syllables of each line, we find they fit the psalter pattern 8686, or common meter. Look at any list of common meter (CM) tunes in the back of your hymnal, and try one of the old psalter tunes. The results are admittedly strange, but not unpleasing.

The worst possible response I can imagine to such a close reading of a hymn text is the accusation that, however clever or not-so-clever, the images and associations I have uncovered are *my* interpretation of the text. That is to say that they are particularly *personal* or that they are somehow esoteric, depending on a load of scholarly knowledge or authority. This accusation would indicate that I have failed to convince readers that these images and associations are natural to the text, that they form a coherent whole picture.

I have tried to ask very commonsensical questions of the words on the page, the sort of questions anybody would ask of a prose text but that we have somehow decided that poetry shouldn't have to answer. I have tried to show how we can answer many of these questions using just a dictionary and our knowledge of familiar Bible stories and expressions. If I have added a measure of information from the poetic tradition—a bit of Shakespeare, Donne, and Milton—I may be forgiven: writing poetry we employ a language conditioned and molded by other poets, carrying their meanings with us, like it or not.

While not every psalm and hymn of Watts is so rich in association or rewards such detailed study, more straightforward texts are no less valuable. The experience of "Joy to the World," like specialized training, prepares us to notice the fine details of other hymns. We can proceed in the confidence that Watts, at least, knew exactly what he was doing.

Our work with "Joy to the World" has also alerted us to the alterations of editors—from the changes in punctuation to the subverting of metaphors to the repetitions that might come with a new tune. Done carefully, such alteration is no violation of an original hymn. Hymns focus and give voice to Christian experience, an experience that changes subtly in time, in a language and to music that change in time. They must naturally adapt. They are performance texts like drama, ever subject to alteration.

O God, Our Help in Ages Past

We turn to examine and compare another very familiar Watts psalm in common meter, "O God, Our Help in Ages Past." (Perhaps you even tried to imagine "Joy to the World" sung to the tune of "O God, Our Help in Ages Past" and found it didn't work because the initial emphasis of this tune falls on the second, rather than the first word.) Psalm 90 begins "Lord, thou hast been our dwelling place." Again, the familiarity of the psalm is part of our experience of the hymn text and must have played an even larger part in the experience of Watts's original singers.

Man Frail and God Eternal

1. Our God, our Help in Ages past,
       Our Hope for Years to come,
    Our Shelter from the stormy Blast,
       And our eternal Home.

2. Under the Shadow of thy Throne
       Thy Saints have dwelt secure;
    Sufficient is thine Arm alone,
       And our Defence is sure.

3. Before the Hills in order stood,
       Or Earth receiv'd her Frame,
    From everlasting Thou art God,
       To endless Years the same.

4. Thy Word commands our Flesh to Dust,
       Return, ye Sons of Men:
    All Nations rose from Earth at first,
       And turn to Earth again.

5. A thousand Ages in thy Sight
   Are like an Evening gone;
   Short as the Watch that ends the Night
   Before the rising Sun.

6. The busy Tribes of Flesh and Blood
   With all their Lives and Cares
   Are carried downwards by thy Flood,
   And lost in following Years.

7. Time like an ever-rolling Stream
   Bears all its Sons away;
   They fly forgotten as a Dream
   Dies at the opening Day.

8. Like flow'ry Fields the Nations stand
   Pleas'd with the Morning-light;
   The Flowers beneath the Mower's Hand
   Ly withering e'er 'tis Night.

9. Our God, our Help in Ages past,
   Our Hope for Years to come,
   Be thou our Guard while Troubles last,
   And our eternal Home.

The critical hymn reader is first struck by the alteration, following John Wesley, of the original "Our God" to "O God" by all but the Presbyterians. This, along with the new colon (Lutheran and Episcopalian) at the end of the stanza, replacing the period, seems to have been an editorial attempt to correct a perceived grammatical lapse on Watts's part. As in the first phrase of "Joy to the World," Watts has given us an incomplete sentence. Editors, including Wesley, have, with their somewhat empty "O God" and their colon, tried to turn the first stanza into an introduction: "O God," our this, our that, our this, our that: "thy saints have dwelt . . ." The original version is more subtle and makes more sense: we begin with a series of simple affirmations of our familiar beliefs about God. By themselves they take us ("Man frail" of the title) nowhere—grammatically or devotionally—until we have examined and animated them. This is the process of the hymn. In the final reworking of these ideas, in the last stanza, we have the verb, the logical integrity we want.

In the first stanza (as Watts wrote it), God is claimed as *our* God no less than five times. The first-person plural possessive pronoun echoes and reechoes while we try out common metaphors that will identify just what God is: help, hope, shelter, home. The message of God as the God of history organizes the first two lines, "Help in Ages past" and "Hope for Years to come"—that's past and future. But, as if expressing our impatience with the standard formulae and their vague underdevelopment, Watts turns us to the more immediate and dramatic metaphor of the psalm. As "Our Shelter from the stormy Blast," God is a very present help. The idea of shelter and our need for it takes us on to eternity and "our eternal Home." The stanza has covered history: past and future, the present and eternity, insisting on our God's presence throughout. The absence of a verb is part of the meaning: our series of claims and metaphors through time is inconclusive, hence incomplete. We are caught up in *our* frail ideas and *our* frail history, which take us nowhere.

In the second stanza, the possessive pronoun *thy* (or *your,* as often updated) takes over, and we (except the Presbyterians, who skip to stanza 3) are moved in the right devotional direction. The metaphor of shelter, introduced in the third line of the preceding stanza, is reworked as evidence of God's protection of the saints through all generations. It's still vague and strange, however, reflecting our frail incomprehension of eternal security: this Throne with its Shadow is mysterious and elevated, however wonderful. The stormy Blast of the previous stanza still echoes in our ears, and we may well wonder how Shadows of Thrones can shelter us from something so immediate and evil. Regardless of *our* doubts—reflected, I like to think, in the relatively abstract and distant language of *secure* and *sufficient,* as well as the Shadows of Thrones—the experience of the Saints in history insists that the security is real. (Methodist editors have, however, resisted, substituting the petition "still may we dwell secure" for the recorded experience of the saints.)

In the second half of the stanza, "thine Arm" as sufficient Defence replaces the image of "thy Throne" as shelter. As a more anthropomorphic metaphor, we expect the arm to be more comforting, but it remains cut off from any sympathetic shoulder, strange and fierce.

It becomes apparent that, in keeping with Watts's title, the effort of the hymn is to give "Frail Man" a glimpse of "God Eternal." Neither our simple metaphors (stanza 1) nor our more elaborate constructs (stanza 2) quite do the trick. The third stanza turns to imagine God before "Ages past," imaginatively pushing back in time before creation. The grammatical construction that permits this idea takes God as subject—for the first time in the hymn: "Thou art God." The present tense of the confessional formula extends from pre-creation past comprehensible time, reflected in the paradox of "endless Years." The metaphorical precision of creation, the personified Hills standing in order, the personified Earth receiving her (or its) frame, contrasts sharply with such a paradox. Our language rebels under the strain of comprehending eternity. (The femaleness of the earth is not an issue here, where the image is one of framing or building rather than fertility.)

The fourth stanza, which is not included in any of our five hymnals, acknowledges the power of *thy* word over a more immediate and knowable creation, our own, the beginning and end of our own mortality. The *Word* which "commands our Flesh to Dust" is, of course, indicative of a fearsome God of life- and death-giving authority, but it has another function as well. This *Word* commands our realization of our mortality (Flesh to Dust), both individual and collective, in the context of God's eternity. Notice Watts's "zoom lens" at work again—zooming in from the eternal, almost incomprehensible time of endless years to mortal time, bounded by birth and death. So, by extension, we understand the birth and death of nations, rising and returning to Earth at the command of the Lord.

Because the fifth stanza builds upon the fourth, we miss it when it is deleted. These are the Ages past (referring back to the first metaphor of the first line) when God has been our Help. The ages are seen as cycles of individual and national birth and death, a thousand of which are, in God's Sight, "like an Evening gone." The anthropomorphic *Word* of God in stanza 4 is similarly a preliminary to the *Sight* of God in stanza 5. We are, under

Watts's direction, experimenting with God's perspective—Arm, Word, Sight. These metaphors are assisted by similes: to God, the ages are *like* an Evening, short *as* the Watch.

With its similes, the fifth stanza introduces the body of the hymn, which weaves together two basic comparisons: (1) the thousand ages are compared to our frail experience of day and night, and (2) time is compared to a rushing river. The "busy Tribes" of stanza 6, with all their limitations, are powerless, dwarfed and caught up by the flood of years. This haunting picture, eliminated, with stanza 6, from all our hymnals, explains the next stanza, retained by all: Time, which is "like an ever-rolling Stream" (stanza 7), is "thy Flood" (stanza 6), God's own eternity. The children of Time, "its Sons," are lost and forgotten. Watts *carefully* avoids identifying the singers with these children. We are, after all, assured of God's Help and Hope and Shelter and eternal Home. Certainly the alterations of stanza 7, according to which Time "*soon* bears *us all* away" (Lutheran, Catholic, and Presbyterian) or "*bears all who breathe* away" (Methodist) and which say "*we* fly forgotten," are distortions. Watts's very careful use of *our* in the first stanza should serve as warning. (The Episcopal version, "Bears all our years away," avoids the issue but doesn't really mean much.)

In the series of similes that make up stanzas 5 through 8 we obtain a series of moral pictures, illustrating ideas of eternity. The Evening gone, the watchers, the busy Tribes, the Flood, the Stream, the dawn, the flow'ry Fields and the Mower in the evening—these are the material of pastoral poetry, nature poetry. Nature is full of such moral pictures, "emblems" of eternity, that, rightly understood, allow us to see our place in the larger picture, our time in the continuum of God's time. Having studied these pictures, we can pray intelligibly, as we do in the final stanza.

Neither *we* nor *our* appear in stanzas 5 through 8 as Watts wrote them (since *our* Flesh was commanded to Dust and we were reminded of our inconsequentiality in stanza 4). We became spectators, watching the pictures of Tribes and Time. Lessoned in eternity, we return, in stanza 9, to the first-person plural *we*.

The exercises in time have provided a context, a perspective, that lets our string of metaphors relate to their subject, revising the first stanza into its final form. The "Ages past" now mean much more, entailing the experience of the Saints, the time before creation, the speedy transience of all life. Please note: God as "our Help" through these Ages has most certainly *not* contemned us, the Saints, as dust, as "busy Tribes of Flesh and Blood," fled "forgotten as a Dream," mown down "Like flow'ry Fields." All our modern versions are misleading, misrepresenting both the situation of "Man Frail" and the nature of "God Eternal." God's "Help" is sure, despite our human frailty; our "Hope" persists despite our realization of our limitations. Now we may petition God intelligibly: "Be thou our Guard." (The Episcopalian and Methodist substitution of *guide* for *guard* is unaccountable.) The present "Troubles," like other mortal things, cannot last long. The idea of "our eternal Home," finally, defies all the evidence of our frail experience. We belong to eternity.

The logical and dramatic tension of the hymn, suggested by the original title, makes it work. The first and last stanzas frame the discussion of what mortality and eternity mean as they demonstrate, with their differences, how we grow in spiritual understanding by contemplating time. This is all a comforting response to Psalm 90, which, for all its beauty, is very disturbing.

II: Watts's Hymns and Spiritual Songs

Turning from Watts's psalms to his hymns, we turn back a dozen years in time, to 1707. We take congregational hymns so for granted that we easily forget the revolutionary achievement of the collection *Hymns and Spiritual Songs*—the first collection of hymns in English that were widely sung and accepted and have continued to define what hymns are up to our day. Watts felt that hymns were needed supplements to the psalter, more capable than the old psalms of expressing specifically Christian devotion. He was conscious that this was a daring innovation and wrote very cautiously. Three well-known hymns treating the Passion of our Lord are, as they treat central Christian experience, particularly representative of *Hymns and Spiritual Songs* and Watts's achievement.*

* *Hymns and Spiritual Songs, 1707–1748* has been edited by Selma L. Bishop (London: The Faith Press, 1962).

Alas! And Did My Saviour Bleed

"Godly Sorrow Arising from the Sufferings of Christ," the original title of "Alas! And Did My Savior Bleed,"the first of these Passion hymns, explains what the hymn is doing. The poetic rehearsal of the sufferings of Christ provokes our sorrowful response, given voice in the verses. The hymn text weaves together recollection of that suffering and directed reaction:

Godly Sorrow arising from the Sufferings of Christ

1. ALass! and did my Saviour bleed,
   And did my Sovereign die?
   Would he devote that sacred Head
   For such a Worm as I?

[2. Thy Body slain, sweet *Jesus,* thine,
   And bath'd in its own Blood,
   While all expos'd to Wrath divine
   The glorious Sufferer stood?]

3. Was it for Crimes that I had done
   He groan'd upon the Tree?
   Amazing Pity! Grace unknown!
   And Love beyond degree!

4. Well might the Sun in Darkness hide,
   And shut his Glories in,
   When God the mighty Maker dy'd
   For Man the Creatures Sin.

5. Thus might I hide my blushing Face
   While his dear Cross appears,
   Dissolve my Heart in Thankfulness,
   And melt my Eyes to Tears.

6. But Drops of Grief can ne'er repay
   The Debt of Love I owe;
   Here, Lord, I give my self away,
   'Tis all that I can do.

The first word of the first stanza gives us pause, not because we don't know what it means, but because it's such an artificial and poetical exclamation of sorrow. What are we doing, Christians in the late twentieth century, beginning one of our important hymns by singing "Alas!"? But before we recommend an alternative, we should consider that perhaps such a standardized and artificial expression of grief is still where we begin our engagement with the sufferings of Christ. The trick is to turn this to real sorrow, responding to the events of Calvary. "Alas" is where we latch on.

Indeed, the strange questions that follow are appropriate to such a challenge: We've come in in the middle of the story, beginning with "and did. . . ." The questions indicate that we're not sure just what's going on here, while the first-person pronouns (*my, my, I*) suggest our involvement in, our ownership of, the experience, whether we understand it or not. There's tension here as each singer claims "my Saviour" and "my Sovereign," while wondering that this—whatever it is—really happened. The heart of the remarkable, even dubious (as indicated by the questioning) idea, which we voice in the next two lines, is the sacrifice of something so terrific—with all the fondness and intimacy of "that sacred Head"—for something worthless, myself, for me as lowly worm.

Almost needless to say, the substitution (in those three hymnals that retain this hymn) of "sinners such as I" for "such a Worm as I" damages the careful voice and balance of imagery Watts has contrived here. "Sinners" are a collective; the Worm is the self, the singular "I." "Sinners such as I" is diluted and abstract. It retreats from immediate realization and confession into categorization, stressing group membership. "Such a Worm" is an immediate and visual counterpart to the sacred Head, full of appropriate self-contempt. The point most certainly *isn't* that Watts thinks he's a worm or that people are all worms—which would indeed call for discreet alteration. The point is that we are, confronted by the Crucifixion, initially filled with powerful disgust and graphic self-loathing.

A word is in order regarding the word *devote* in the line "Would he devote that sacred Head." Obvious meanings include "dedicate" or "give up for the benefit of," properly suggesting willing sacrifice. A more obscure meaning is also powerful, especially with reference to the worm (itself an archaic term for Satan). *Devote* can also mean to "consign to powers of evil" or "give over to destruction." Here he dooms his sacred head for the worm, the "I" who has just dared question whether he "would" do such a thing. Poetry allows these multiple meanings and encourages us to explore them.

In the second stanza, stricken from all three hymnals, the first-person pronoun *(I)* is gone, and we have, under the guise of a continued question, a discomfortingly vivid picture. The heightened discomfort is part of the calculated effect, a turning of the tension screw, part of what the hymn is to do to us as it expresses the "Godly Sorrow arising from the Sufferings of Christ." "Thy Body slain . . . and bathed in its own Blood . . . all expos'd" is horrible, as it should be. The "Wrath divine," to which Jesus is willingly subject, is frightening. The interjection in the first line, "Sweet Jesus," tender and even diminutive (in contrast to Saviour and Sovereign), jolts us, a forceful reminder of our love for this sacrificial victim. Finally, in the paradoxical image of the "Glorious Sufferer," the basic contradiction of the glory of God and the pain of Christ is summarized. The glory and the suffering are extraordinary, unaccountable, unprecedented partners—the contradiction by means of which we imagine the meaning of the Son of God crucified.

In the third stanza, we ask the final question and turn to concentrate on our response, which has only been suggested through the course of the first two stanzas. The final question—by now rhetorical and answered, like the others, in the affirmative—is the crux: Was it my fault? "Was it for Crimes that I had done / He groan'd upon the Tree?" We have learned that yes is the right answer. We note the moaning sounds of *done* and *groan'd* and *upon* and may regret the Presbyterian substitution of *suffered* for *groaned.* We note as well another doubtful substitution: Lutherans and Presbyterians both replace *Crimes* with *sins.* The Crucifixion as a violent punishment for crimes Jesus didn't commit but we did is the point. *Sins* is relatively weak and abstract. We may, like our eighteenth-century forbears, need help understanding sin. Crime—in the streets, on television, in our nightmares—is very familiar. Indeed, the dramatic, unavoidable realization, here in the third stanza, that we are all involved, is part of the curve of the hymn, its response "arising," in the terminology of the title. It should not be moderated or theologized.

Our reaction, following this realization of how we are implicated, is absolute astonishment, indicated by the altered punctuation, the switch from question marks to exclamation points (except in the Lutheran version). Let's appreciate the original knockout power of *amazing*, which we moderns have overused and cheapened (along with *awesome* and *wonderful*). "Pity," familiar to each of us as a mild and teary sentiment, ascribed to Christ, is understood as "amazing," filling us with wonder at its extent. This is how anthropomorphic metaphors work. They begin with simple comparisons, grounded in experience—our experience of familiar pity, familiar grace and love, as initial means of understanding, as step one. These metaphors, in a good poem, are then imaginatively extended to the unknowable, exploded, as it were. So the Grace is "unknown," incomprehensible to humans, yet acknowledged, and so the Love is "beyond degree," i.e., extrapolated beyond measure.

In the fourth stanza, created nature's response to the Crucifixion is understood as appropriate. It will become a model for our own sorrow. The Sun hides his glories in darkness as the Son, the "glorious Sufferer" of stanza 2, has hidden his glories in suffering and death. This conventional pun, identifying the Son with the sun and its light and life and setting and rising, is rich in association. (The masculine *his*, removed from all three hymnals, had reinforced the association.) The power of the paradox is driven home in the second pair of lines: the Maker's death marks a shameful inversion of right relations between Creator and created things, an embarrassment. (When the Presbyterians revised the third line to read "When Christ, the great Redeemer died," they missed the creation idea basic to the stanza.) The shame prepares us for the blushing to come.

The rationale for the Lutheran alteration of "Man the Creatures Sin" to "his own creatures' sin" is problematic. "God the mighty Maker" had been carefully juxtaposed to "Man the Creature," defining the relationship between God and the individual human. (Several early editions of the hymn place an apostrophe in the singular, possessive position.) The alteration, as it introduces a plural *(sinners')*, knocks out the parallel, diffuses the individual focus on the self (important since the first line and throughout the hymn), and adds a new and unnecessarily masculine pronoun for God! The Methodist "his own creature's sin" avoids the plural but still inserts the masculine pronoun. In a conservative mood, I would advise the return to Watts's original, arguing that "Man the creature" clearly explains itself as not the male sex. In a more liberal mood, I would recommend "for my, a creature's, sin." I might compromise on "For human creature's Sin." (That would mean simply moving the apostrophe in the Presbyterian version, "For human creatures' sin.")

In the fifth stanza, the singer's sorrow is modeled. "I" *should properly* (i.e., "well might I") emulate the Sun of the preceding stanza, hiding my "blushing Face" as the Sun hid his "glories" as the Son suffered, all in profound embarrassment. Blushes also suggest lovers' behavior, and the appearance of the "dear Cross," taken with the "Love beyond degree" of "sweet Jesus" indicates a pattern of love language. This is one of those analogies, one of those patterns of metaphor, built into the language, that connects orders of experience we would, timidly and ascetically, prefer to keep apart. Our embarrassment, Watts indicates, is as strong and as physical as that of mortal lovers. (Presbyterians don't sing stanza 5.)

The blushing face, the heart dissolving, the melted, weeping eyes— "well might" the "Godly Sorrow" grip us *physically*. If it fails to do so, we are less responsive than the Sun. This strong response is perfectly appropriate. We note, however, that however strong, *it is no subjective-expressive-spontaneous overflow of Watts's emotions* on the page, but rather a description of feelings proper to human creatures contemplating the Cross. It is a devotional exercise, carefully directed in the manner of the spiritual exercises of Ignatius Loyola.

The last stanza corrects any tendency we might exhibit to settle for purely emotional response, however appropriate. Such blushes and dissolvings and tears are insufficient. The only right response is the offering up of the self. "Drops of Grief," like drops of anything, are insignificant, however plentiful. (The Lutheran-Methodist substitution of "tears of grief" seems a loss.) The original "can ne'er," unlike the altered "cannot," suggests continued effort at tearful repayment. Our tears can *never* ("ne'er") pay this debt, but we will keep weeping. (Tears as coins for payment are possibly also a subtle reference to John Donne's great poem "A Valediction," where tears are valuable only because they bear the image of the beloved.)

This realization of the ultimate insufficiency of even the holiest of human "Godly sorrow" marks the completion of the process of the hymn. We are enabled, through this process, to turn, at last, to address the Lord for the first time in the hymn. This is its achievement. The Saviour's devotion of his head, his payment for my crimes, all amazing, unknown, beyond degree, lead, in the end, to my own giving of my *self* (*not* the reflexive "myself" of the hymnal versions). This is beyond blushing and weeping. It is "all" I can do in two meanings—*all* as modest ("I'm afraid that's all I can do") and *all* as total ("I give my self, my all, away").

It Happened on That Fateful Night

Only the Lutherans have included the next hymn, "The Lord's Supper Instituted," in their hymnal (found there as "It Happened on That Fateful Night"). The original refers us to "I Corinthians 11.23 &c.," the words of institution. Here, we turn from the modeling of highly individual response, the task of "Godly Sorrow arising," to the dramatic recreation of the Lord's Supper (stanzas 1–3). This is followed by the collective response of the communicants (stanzas 4–7). "I," "me," and "my" are notably absent here, while "For us" is carefully emphasized at the beginning of stanzas 3 and 4.

The Lord's Supper Instituted

1.   'TWAS on that dark, that doleful Night
     When Powers of Earth and Hell arose
     Against the Son of God's Delight,
     And Friends betray'd him to his Foes:

2. Before the mournful Scene began
   He took the Bread, and blest, and brake:
   What Love thro' all his Actions ran!
   What wond'rous Words of Grace he spake!

3. *This is my Body broke for Sin,*
   Receive and eat the living Food:
   Then took the Cup, and blest the Wine;
   'Tis the New Cov'nant in my Blood.

[4. For us his Flesh with Nails was torn,
   He bore the Scourge, he felt the Thorn;
   And Justice pour'd upon his Head
   Its heavy Vengeance in our stead.

5. For us his vital Blood was spilt,
   To buy the Pardon of our Guilt,
   When for black Crimes of biggest Size
   He gave his Soul a Sacrifice.]

6. *Do this* (he cry'd) *till Time shall end,*
   In Memory of your dying Friend;
   Meet at my Table, and record
   The Love of your departed Lord.

7. *Jesus,* thy Feast we celebrate,
   We show thy Death, we sing thy Name,
   Till thou return, and we shall eat
   The Marriage-Supper of the Lamb.

The first two lines of the first stanza set the scene, self-consciously spooky, something like a Halloween story. Familiar stories often begin with the "'Twas" formula ("'Twas the Night before Christmas"), and Halloween is, after all, when we summon up dark nights and the powers of earth and hell. *Dark* and *doleful* are linked by alliteration, with *doleful* a fine, primitive word, suggesting all things woeful and lamentable, cheerless and gloomy. The *dole* is also a gift, distributed as charity, so the night of the Supper is "doleful" in a second sense, full of giving to the miserable. The Latin verb *dolere* means "to suffer or grieve," indicating that the evening was also full of sorrow. Finally, *dole* can, in the law, mean criminal malice. Indeed, the night was one full of criminal malice. Certainly the Lutheran substitution of "It happened on that *fateful* night" suggests the wrong idea entirely: the events of Maundy Thursday were not "fated" in any useful sense of the word.

The "Powers" who rise in this story are active and threatening, subverting "the Son of God's Delight." Jesus' pleasure is indeed under siege, but De*light* also suggests light, the light of heaven, the light of creation, the light of the world, the Sun (Son), sabotaged by the *dark* powers of earth and hell. There's a cosmic battle being waged here and the hymn opens as an adventure story. We note the meaning lost in the Lutheran alteration to "the Son, our God's delight" and its confusing possessive: the original indeed suggests that the Son is God's delight, but that is only one of several meanings—and not even the most important.

In the second stanza, the stage having been set and the characters having been introduced, Watts is explicit about the nature of his hymn task, the dramatic reconstruction of the events of Holy Thursday. The institution of the Supper is basically anticipatory; it comes "before" the "mournful Scene" that was to follow, all the while garnering its significance from what follows. The time order is thus crucial: the betrayal and suffering and death that are to come, not the Supper itself, are the "mournful Scene." This idea is quite different from, and much more suggestive and precise than, the "bitter scene" of the Lutheran hymnal. We mourn our sins as well as our dead. The appropriate mood before such a scene is grief and melancholy, not bitterness. As usual, Watts tells us exactly how to respond.

With tight dramatic control, Watts begins the institution ("He took the Bread, and blest, and brake") and then suspends it, injecting two exclamations, model observations for us to sing about the action. It is animated by love: "What love thro' all his Actions ran!" And the words communicate grace: "What wond'rous Words of Grace he spake!" Under Watts's direction we pause to reflect on the activity recreated before us. We know exactly what is coming, but it's remarkable nonetheless. Rarely, and only with great precision and such dramatic control, do hymns have us sing the words of Christ, particularly words spoken by ministers in their priestly capacity.

The following two stanzas explain the Body and Blood of stanza 3, the elements of the meal that can only be understood with reference to the subsequent "mournful Scene." That's an important part of our processing those words of the hymn, just as it's an important item in our understanding the sacrament: the hymn is working in a way analogous to the sacrament as memorial. The Supper makes us recall the events to come and their purpose ("For us . . . for us . . ."). The "Flesh . . . torn" is the same "Body broke," the "living Food," we have just sung of. That figure whose actions were animated by love is the same who "bore the Scourge" and "felt the Thorn." The "Justice pour'd upon his Head" refers us, with its "pouring," back to the cup, "the New Cov'nant." In stanza 5, the Blood, as "vital," is both essential and living. A lovely word, *vital* has such implications. "Our Guilt" lines us up with those traitorous "Friends" of the first stanza, whose immense "black Crimes" are the materials of the adventure story.

No idle digression, these stanzas, inserted in the words of institution, are structurally important and teach us about the way hymns form our response, knitting up patterns of association and meaning. These stanzas, as they tie together the events of Thursday night and Friday with our own experience of the sacrament, belong right where they are. (They are stricken from the Lutheran version.)

With this commentary, we have become involved in the sacrament, its institution "For us" and its purpose. We return, in stanza 6, to the words of institution, rather daringly revised with heightened dramatic effects. The "Memory of your dying Friend," intimate and strongly appealing, is carefully balanced against the more lofty and formal "The Love of your departed Lord." "*Meet* at my Table" is possibly a modest Baroque pun (the dying Friend as meat, meaning "food"). We can only marvel that the word *record*, meaning to recall or remember, has not been touched by the generally cruel hand of "Alt." It's a lovely Latinate idea, suggesting to hold in the heart; however, in this sense it is obsolete beyond recall and probably *should* be altered. (If we think *record* means "write down," we miss the point.)

The final stanza summarizes the achievement of the hymn in several ways. For the first time, we address Jesus directly. *Thou* and *thy* are repeated four times in as many lines. The hymn has led us from adventure story to this direct prayer; it has taught us to pray. When we affirm that we celebrate the feast, we mean we do so both in the singing of the hymn and in the celebration of the sacrament. This is explained in the second line, this celebration which includes both "showing" Jesus' death and "singing" Jesus' name. *Show*, like *record* in the previous stanza, is used in its archaic sense of announcing or communicating, as in the legal "show cause." It also suggests performance or display, a public spectacle, apropos the drama of the hymn and the public ritual of communion. In the final two lines, the activity of song and communion is extended into the future, reaching on to the eschaton.

When I Survey the Wondrous Cross

The third, and doubtless the best, of Watts's hymns on the Passion is the "Crucifixion to the World by the Cross of Christ." Reproduced in all five of our hymnals as "When I Survey the Wondrous Cross," the hymn is based on Galatians 6:14: "But far be it from me to glory except in the cross of our Lord Jesus Christ, by which the world has been crucified to me, and I to the world." The basic idea is that we share in the Crucifixion as it radically transforms our understanding of the world. Because of its especially fine detail, we print it here stanza by stanza.

Crucifixion to the World by the Cross of Christ

1. WHen I survey the wond'rous Cross
    On which the Prince of Glory dy'd,
    My richest Gain I count but Loss,
    And pour Contempt on all my Pride.

The initial stanza introduces the main idea, that the view of the Cross reorders our values. The grammar is basic (when I . . . then I) and deceptively simple. In the first two lines, "wond'rous Cross" and "Prince of Glory" give us general ideas rather than sharp pictures. As we noted with "Alas! And Did My Saviour Bleed," such vague and general ideas are where we begin our lessons in Watts's classroom. The subtler details call for our dictionary. While it slips easily by, *survey* is packed with suggestion: to survey is to describe, to observe, to measure. It suggests linear and angular measurement, appropriate to a cross, a scientific, critical inspection. (When the Episcopalians change the second line to read "Where the young Prince of glory died," they lose the exactness of *on which*. The youth of the Prince seems simply odd.) The third and fourth lines are more impressive, intentionally so, as the words demonstrate—as their relations to one another accumulate on the page—the proper response of the believer.

By now I think we understand how the "I" of the hymn is each of us as we should be, should think, should feel. This is the "exemplary I" whose role we each play, learning by expressing perfect faith. Surveying the Cross, I describe my transformed values in an economic metaphor, immediately tied into a moral metaphor. The Bible provides ample precedent for such an association, an association that we return to over and again in the course of the hymn. What I had valued highly, "my richest Gain," is, in this new accounting, a total "Loss." The image of rich gain recalls that of the Prince of Glory; the evaluative activity of counting recalls that of surveying; "Loss" takes us back to "Cross"—our gain, Jesus' loss.

This pattern of cross-reference and recollection becomes even more intricate in the fourth line. The activity of "pouring Contempt" on "Pride" dramatizes mental process: pride drenched, doused with the cold liquid of contempt, is even comical, the stuff of slapstick. The liquid pouring also anticipates the flowing to come in the gripping tableau of the Cross in stanzas 3 and 4—the quantities of blood. *Pour* Contempt further suggests a double meaning to the ear as *Poor* Contempt recalls the economic "Loss" and contrasts with "richest gain" of the preceding line. Just so, the quantity and quantification of Pride, suggested in "all my Pride," recalls the measuring activities of surveying and counting.

The pattern sets up a very important, if subtle, countermovement. When I look at the Cross, I don't understand. I have "My richest Gain" all wrong. It is, in fact, the Cross, which I, confused as I am, "count but Loss."

I can initially see only ruin, devastation, bankruptcy. Just so, "the Prince of Glory" is properly "all my Pride." But I, as a participant in the Crucifixion, "pour Contempt" on him. Here at the start my responses are all wrong. These lines thus mean two very different things, each complete and true at the same time.

The first two lines of the second stanza are an interjection, a little prayer addressed to the Lord in language close to the Galatians text:

> 2. Forbid it, Lord, that I should boast
> Save in the Death of *Christ* my God;
> All the vain things that charm me most,
> I sacrifice them to his Blood.

But look how loaded that language has already become. In this position, following my public announcement of how my values have been reordered by the view of the Cross, the little prayer "Forbid it, Lord, that I should boast" suggests the danger of pride in piety, suggests that what we have been doing, however seemingly innocent, is boasting, and not in the Cross but in our devotional achievements, in our reordered values and doused pride. (The sense of the wrongness of boasting in material achievements, of course, remains.) The second stanza reworks the items of the first, advancing our understanding, preparing us for the coming view of the Cross.

The sacrifice of vanities in lines 3 and 4 of the second stanza is our actual starting point, a necessary preliminary. "*All* the vain things" refers us back to "*all* my Pride" and ahead to the much more comprehensive "All" of the last stanza. "Vain" things rhyme with richest "Gain" in the preceding stanza, and vanity is what generally leads to the forbidden "boasting." "Things" are at once quantifiable (as in "count" and "loss," above) and nonspecific, hence inconsequential. That I am "charmed" by these vain things suggests both my pleasure and my enchantment by them (as magical "charms"), even that they are objects of idolatry, hence suitably sacrificed. Such a sacrifice, however righteous, however a necessary preparation to the exprience of Calvary, is, as the hymn demonstrates, ultimately inadequate as response.

It is the Blood to which I sacrifice that clears my eyes and lets me see and understand. The blood of Christ is both the means of redemption *in absolute theological terms* and the means of advance *in the poetry of the hymn.* When my vanities are sacrificed to "his Blood," suddenly I see and understand the Cross. When Blood, the first substantial, physical material of the hymn, appears at the end of stanza 2, I am allowed my vision of the Crucifixion:

> 3. See from his Head, his Hands, his Feet,
>   Sorrow and Love flow mingled down;
>   Did e're such Love and Sorrow meet?
>   Or Thorns compose so rich a Crown?

In hymn language we do well to take injunctions to "See!" "Hark!" "Behold!" seriously. They signal the introduction of evidence, a scene or a song created for our edification. In contrast to the general "survey" of "the wondrous Cross" with which we began, the bloody vision of the Crucifixion is precise, yet finely restrained. The seeing eye moves from head to hands to feet, following the downward flow of mingled "Sorrow and Love." (When all five hymnals plug in a comma following *See,* they break the "flow" of words, part of Watts's demonstration of what's going on.) We expect blood, since that's what it's all about. The blood as Sorrow and Love surprises us and teaches us, arresting our attention and directing us back from the physical, touchable facts—of blood, head, hands, feet—to their meaning.

After all, it is this meaning for us of the blood as sorrow and love that touches us and moves us, provoking the wondering questions of the balance of the stanza. Blood without such associations is simply clinical, a bodily fluid. The *mingling* of "Sorrow and Love," their twining together, is illustrated in the language of the next line, where their order is reversed to "Love and Sorrow." This twining pattern is also the pattern of the thorns that "compose" the crown. By ignoring the first question mark, it is even possible to hear these lines say something quite different: that the Love and Sorrow are "meet" (or "fitting") and are part of the crown of thorns. With these questions we begin at the foot of the Cross, the meeting place of the sorrow and love. Love and sorrow we know from experience. But here, quite exactly, they are a liquid pool of redeeming blood. Flowing from the body of the crucified Lord, the love and sorrow are both his and ours. We participate in the Crucifixion.

In the last line of the stanza, the "rich Crown" refers us back to the Prince of Glory, the richest gain, the economics of the first stanza. Acknowledgment that thorns should compose so *rich a crown* demonstrates the proper inversion of values. Turning from the pool of blood to the crown, we also raise our eyes back upward. As the Blood at the end of stanza 2 was the cue word for the following stanza, so the Crown at the end of stanza 3 introduces the vitally important stanza 4 (lamentably excised from all five modern hymnals):

> 4. His dying Crimson like a Robe
>   Spreads o're his Body on the Tree,
>   Then am I dead to all the Globe,
>   And all the Globe is dead to me.

Crowns and crimson robes are royal. So is the "Globe" in one of its meanings, "a golden ball carried by sovereigns as an emblem of authority," the ball familiar from countless Renaissance paintings of the Christchild. In stanza 4, Watts draws on such iconography as well as on the Baroque tradition of strong and violent bloody imagery, meant to disturb us. However violent the image of Christ's body dressed in crimson blood may seem, it is restrained and modest set next to Richard Crashaw's lines "On Our Crucified Lord, Naked and Bloody"[*]—or the standard fare at the local movie theater. The crimson of the robe is "dying" in two senses, of course: the blood of a dying man is *dying,* but it is also a spreading *dye.*

The reaction of the singer to this vision is even more violent than to the preceding blood as "Love and Sorrow." This is the climactic "Crucifixion to the World" of the title. The singer "blacks out," loses consciousness, "dead

---

[*]   Th'have left thee naked, Lord, O that they had!
      This garment, too, I would they had denied;
      Thee with thyself they have too richly clad,
      Opening the purple wardrobe of thy side.
          O never could be found garments too good
          For thee to wear, but these, of thy own blood.

to the Globe," just at the moment the darkness descends on nature. The identification with the death of Christ is that personal. (Perhaps a surrealist filmmaker or theatrical producer might attempt the same effect using red gelatin and fading light.) While the state of being "dead to the world" is a loss of consciousness, it is also a metaphor, suggesting total indifference to worldly concerns. This meaning comes through the second statement, subtly different, that "all the Globe is dead to me." The utter desolation of the Globe is brought home.

The final stanza steps back from this profound experience of the Cross and reflects upon it, using words that the prior stanzas have loaded with meaning:

> 5. Were the whole Realm of Nature mine,
>   That were a Present far to[o] small;
>   Love so amazing, so divine
>   Demands my Soul, my Life, my All.

The first line is conditional: "Were the whole Realm of Nature mine." Obviously, it isn't at all. I don't presume to rule the world. Realm has been identified with the Prince of Glory, crowned in thorns and robed in crimson. The Realm of Nature is, moreover, not only not mine, it is dead to me. But if it *were* mine, it would be insufficient as a "Present," or sacrifice, an offering (Episcopal and Methodist)—but most certainly *not* a "tribute" (Lutheran). If the whole world is insufficient, certainly those vain things that charm me, sacrificed, are "far too small." The demand is, rather, for total dedication of "my Soul, my Life, my All."

The unavoidable conclusion is that "my Soul, my Life, my All" are a more worthy gift than the whole world, were it mine to give. And indeed, the idea of giving the Lord the "whole Realm of Nature" was an idle imagining, sprung from "all my Pride," imagining myself as sovereign. We are raised above the realm of nature through our meditation on the Cross. Only through such redeeming elevation can (to return to Paul's words) the world be "crucified to me and I to the world."

III: Charles Wesley's Different Song

M any volumes of hymnology have been devoted to the history, the structure, and the theology of Charles Wesley's (1707–1788) many hymns. For the most part—in keeping with our goal of simple reading—we shall set these studies aside and merely read selected texts. Several features of Wesley's work, however, help us appreciate their difference and so guide our reading:

1. Wesley's hymns belong to the phenomenon of the eighteenth-century evangelical revival, the powerful mass movement that swept Britain and America. Evangelists traveled from community to community, preaching salvation and urging a profoundly personal conversion. This experience of charismatic spirituality naturally informs Wesleyan hymnody.

2. During the lives of the Wesley brothers, the revival took place, for the most part, outside the established church. The Methodist hymn books were one of the means for forming and shaping the common experience of the revival. To this extent they are dogmatic.

3. While we know many of them as congregational hymns, they were originally written to be sung outside of church services, in a religious world apart from liturgical celebration and often in communities that were relatively unstable and often socially marginal. The congregational sense is thus usually absent.

4. The revival emphasis on religious enthusiasm, the stirring of the heart which was to culminate in profound conversion, directed Methodist hymnody, enlisting hymns in the conversion process.

5. Charles Wesley wrote easily and often, producing an estimated seven thousand hymns for an audience that was, in comparison to that of Watts, uneducated and uncritical. This facility might be expected to mar much of his work.

6. The Wesleys successfully encouraged the development and importation of new music, breaking hymnody out of the psalter mode and introducing new metrical options along with rich new melodies. (The extraliturgical place of Methodist hymns helped make this possible.)

In this chapter we shall examine three well-loved hymns by Charles Wesley that have been heavily altered and cut. The originals are available in Frank Baker's *Representative Verse of Charles Wesley* (London: Epworth Press, 1962). The quantity and scope of the alterations suggests original problems, both weaknesses in the poetry and idiosyncrasies of the original revival experience that need translation for modern singers. I may hope that these readings are studied in the generous spirit in which they are offered, a spirit of real respect for hymns and for the life and ministry of Wesley. If I seem harsh, I proceed in confidence that, if I am wrong, I might provoke debate which will serve to sharpen our collective critical understanding. (We'll sample Wesley's better texts in the next chapter.)

Charles Wesley's Different Song

Hark! The Herald Angels Sing

"Hark! The Herald Angels Sing" first appeared in the following form in a 1739 collection as a "Hymn for Christmas Day." As we know it, the first six stanzas have been paired into three and the last four stanzas (7–10) have been cut:

Hymn for Christmas Day

Original

Modern Composite
(alterations in italics)

1. Hark how all the Welkin rings
   "Glory to the King of Kings,
   "Peace on Earth, and Mercy mild,
   "GOD and Sinners reconcil'd!

1. Hark! *The herald angels sing,*
   "Glory to the *newborn King;*
   Peace on earth, and mercy mild,
   God and sinners reconciled."
   Joyful, all you nations rise;
   Join the triumph of the skies;

2. Joyful all ye Nations rise,
   Join the Triumph of the Skies,
   Universal Nature say
   "CHRIST the LORD is born to Day!

   With angelic hosts proclaim,
   "Christ is born in Bethlehem!"
   R: Hark! *The herald angels sing,*
   "Glory to the *newborn King!"*

3. CHRIST, by highest Heav'n ador'd,
   CHRIST, the Everlasting Lord,
   Late in Time behold him come,
   Offspring of a Virgin's Womb.

2. Christ, by highest heav'n adored,
   Christ, the everlasting Lord,
   Late in time behold him come,
   Offspring of a virgin's womb.
   Veiled in flesh the Godhead see!
   Hail, th' incarnate deity!

4. Veil'd in Flesh, the Godhead see,
   Hail th'Incarnate Deity!
   Pleas'd as Man with Men t'appear
   JESUS, our *Immanuel* here!

   Pleased as man with *us to dwell,*
   Jesus, our Emmanuel!
   R: Hark! The herald angels sing,
   "Glory to the *newborn King!"*

5. Hail the Heav'nly Prince of Peace!

3. Hail the *heav'n-born* Prince of Peace!

   Hail the Sun of Righteousness!

   Hail the sun of righteousness!

47

Light and Life to All he brings,
Ris'n with Healing in his Wings.

Light and life to all he brings,
Ris'n with healing in his wings.
Mild he lays his glory by,
Born that *we* no more may die,
Born to raise *each child* of earth,
Born to give *us* second birth.
R: Hark! The herald angels sing,
   "Glory to the *newborn King!*"

6. Mild he lays his Glory by,
   Born—that Man no more may die,
   Born—to raise the Sons of Earth,
   Born—to give them Second Birth.

7. Come, Desire of Nations, come,
   Fix in Us thy humble Home,
   Rise, the Woman's Conqu'ring Seed,
   Bruise in Us the Serpent's Head.

(eliminated)

8. Now display thy saving Pow'r,
   Ruin'd Nature now restore,
   Now in Mystic Union join
   Thine to Ours, and Ours to Thine.

(eliminated)

9. *Adam's* Likeness, LORD, efface,
   Stamp thy Image in its Place,
   Second *Adam* from above,
   Reinstate us in thy Love.

(eliminated)

10. Let us Thee, tho' lost, regain,
   Thee, the Life, the Inner Man:
   O! to All Thyself impart,
   Form'd in each Believing Heart.

(eliminated)

The first striking feature of this text as a new kind of hymn is its metrics. Each line contains seven syllables, indicating how the molds of metrical psalmody were cracking. The pattern of emphases is also new, as every line begins with an accented syllable. Seven-syllable lines made this possible: since the natural rhythm of English alternates stressed and unstressed syllables and most of our rhymes are so-called masculine rhymes, hymn lines of even-numbered syllables (6, 8) tend to begin with a weak beat. A line that begins with a strong beat sounds assertive, insistent. The grouping of the lines into the eight-line stanzas of the hymn as we know it is a further novelty, ideally permitting more sustained thought. Finally, we observe that the rhymes are different, pairing lines in couplets (*aa, bb, cc,* etc.) rather than alternating (*abab, cdcd,* etc.). Such pairing tends to break up the thought of a stanza into two-line units.

Ignoring, for the moment, the refrain, which wasn't in the original text, this hymn is best understood as a series of commands: Hark! Rise! Behold! See! Hail! Hail! Hail! The hymn conjures up the experience of a crowd of people who hear a parade or royal procession advancing. The herald angels announce the event. The nations respond by rising to their feet. Then they join in the singing. In the second stanza, Christ actually comes into view ("behold him come") and we can "see" what we have expected and risen to meet. The final stage is the "hailing" of this new king for all he represents. The emphatic meter enforces the commands, while the excitement of the crowd, the rush of Christmas high spirits, is evident in the sometime unintelligibility of what we are commanded to hear, to see, and to do.

Turning to study the familiar words on the page in close detail, and to compare them with the original, we may well be puzzled. Royal processions and crowd activity (particularly hailing kings) are a bit removed from our experience. There's also a real rush of ideas here, so much happening, not all of it very clear. Take the opening archaism, for example. *Hark!* has lost almost all its meaning as an injunction to *Listen!*—so much so that it may well slip out of our lips on Christmas like so much nonsense, nonsense repeated in the refrain. The musical emphases don't help as they force together the harking and the angels. I think the mind's ear, regardless of punctuation and quotation marks (deleted by the Episcopalians), may even tend to hear *Hark* as *what* the herald angels sing (if the mind's ear ever gets the idea of angels as "heralds," announcing the royal advance). In Wesley's original the *hark* was linked reasonably to what followed, which we would paraphrase as, "Listen how all the vault of heaven rings. . . ." While the *Welkin* of the original was obscure and needed alteration, and *herald angels* fit the basic story of the hymn nicely, the modern version is unnecessarily confusing.

The archaic unfamiliarity of *Hark!* is, however, only a part of a larger problem. Wesley was possibly trying to do too many things in his first stanza. He has his singers tell others to "Listen," then to quote what they hear—a kind of crazy jumble, to be frank, of glory and peace and mercy and reconciliation. All hint at reasons for glory, but they sit there undeveloped and unrelated to one another: the "Glory to the newborn King" is not clearly tied to "Peace on Earth." Is this a related item to glorify (as indicated in the punctuation of the original), somehow a separate angelic command (as in "Let there be peace on earth"), or an announcement, taken with "mercy mild"? It's simply not clear. Nor does the fourth line come clear. How do these items, each suggesting relationships, cohere? (If they don't and never did, what does this signify about the meaning and function of hymnody?)

In the second four-line unit, we-as-singers command the nations, who have presumably heard the angels, to "rise." Like spectators at a royal procession (the "triumph" of the next line, unfortunately an archaism), the joyful nations are told to rise to their feet, then to "join" the angelic acclamation and to "proclaim" the good news with the angels. (The crowd scenes of the revival come to mind.) This progression of commanded response makes good sense, logical and coherent, until we come to the refrain. It isn't right to return to the heralds and our initial hearkening! The procession is well underway by this point, the heralds are on down the road. We have risen to see what's coming.

The refrain is further problematic as it insists on this parade as an honor paid to the "*newborn* King." If you review the original, you see how the *royalty* rather than the *infancy* of Jesus is the main point. The angels sing "Glory to the King of Kings," and, while his birth is indeed proclaimed, it is the mature Christ who comes into view in the procession, not a venerated baby. The baby, for all its importance, doesn't fit with the tableau that is unfolding before our eyes, the public event we are commanded to participate in.

In the next stanza the commanding verbs are *behold* and *see*. These commands generally signal an important hymn spectacle, the visual focus of a hymn-as-entertainment. Forcing together heavenly adoration, everlasting authority, latter day history, and the virgin birth, Wesley's spectacle is obscure. We're not sure what we are to "behold." Further confusion comes with the injunction "Veiled in flesh the Godhead see!" When Godhead is veiled in flesh the whole point would seem to be that we cannot see it. What are we looking at? Why are we so excited?

The following lines command our adoring response, our "hailing." This is another problematic archaism as few of us have ever really hailed anything but a taxi. We are left to learn what hailing is by doing it in such a hymn, and here it seems a kind of incantatory process: we "hail" the "incarnate deity"—rather an abstract and Latinate concept, modified by Jesus' "pleasure" at joining us. This pleasure—"Pleased as man with us to dwell"—had real possibilities as a ground for our admiration, possibilities Wesley characteristically failed to develop. (The modern Methodist—"with us in flesh"—and Presbyterian—"in flesh with us"—versions fiddle with the relationship, trying to make sense of the fleshly veil. Wesley seemed more concerned, for the moment, with the Emmanuel idea—God with us.)

In the following stanza we note the alteration of "Heav'nly Prince of Peace" to "heav'n-born Prince of Peace." I suspect that most singers are completely lost and confused by this point in the hymn, or else totally carried away by the simple joys of song. How otherwise can we explain this "heav'n-born Prince"? The whole point of Christmas would seem to be the birth of the Prince at Bethlehem, very much on this earth. *Heav'n-born* is unhelpful at best (although familiar from Milton's Nativity poem).

With Jesus as the "sun of righteousness," bringing light and life to all, Wesley invokes the powerful traditional association between the sun and the Son. Hailing the rising sun is a fine traditional poetic activity, familiar from the *aubade,* or morning song. In the following two lines, which are, remarkably, the first declarative sentence of the hymn, he attempts to sustain and develop this image and almost immediately gets into trouble: "Light and life to all he brings" explains the sun/Son analogy. "Ris'n with healing in his wings," however biblical (Malachi 4:2), gets terribly confusing. We are already coping with "heaven-born" and the life-giving metaphor of the Son as sun. The added strain of wings is unbearable. How can we picture the Prince-of-Peace-as-Son as sun-as-winged, these wings, moreover, somehow *containing* healing as he rises?

In the following lines, where this winged figure sets aside his glory to be born, the metaphor gets in even worse trouble. The mainspring of the sun/Son analogy is usually the Resurrection. Here we seem to be going back to the conception of Jesus, where he laid his glory by. But then why have we been singing "Glory to the newborn King" over and over? And what happened to the procession?

The purposes of that birth, sketched in the three lines beginning with *Born,* seem like a kind of puzzling rhetorical play. In our modern versions (except the Episcopalian) they are the finale, leaving us with a sense of having gotten lost along the way. In Wesley's original they introduce the second half of the hymn with its rush of ideas. While he toys with the polarities of Jesus' birth and our death, he assumes considerable theological understanding necessary to appreciate how Jesus was born "that man/we no more may die." But we are rushed on. His birth "to raise the Sons of Earth" has terrific potential: it might take us back to the sun as source of light and life and the idea of raising crops, or it might suggest a child-rearing analogy. But the potential is undeveloped, and, I suspect, few singers make anything of the lines beyond a vague idea of our salvation for which Jesus was born. The common (GIA, Methodist, and Presbyterian) alteration "born to raise us from the earth," jumbles together creation with levitation and resurrection. We rush on to our second birth, another undeveloped idea, however fertile. (In a fine attempt to order the wild rush of ideas, the Episcopalian version of the last stanza revises Wesley's stanzas 5 and 6. The "Born" lines thus follow the Incarnation lines of Wesley's stanza 4, which makes sense. The Episcopalians then run the lines of Wesley's stanza 5 in reverse order—risen with healing, light and life, then concluding with the "hailing," a subtle pun on *healing.* However radical, the alteration works well.)

The hymn as we have it ends here. As Wesley wrote it, the rush of ideas gets wilder and wilder. The processional is forgotten. The singers no longer address the nations but rather command the Lord to "Come . . . Fix . . . Rise . . . Bruise," to "display . . . restore . . . join . . . efface . . . stamp . . . reinstate." The metaphors are tossed out and abandoned in this rush: the desire of nations, humble homes, conquering seed, serpent's head, power, ruined nature, mystic union, and so on. We may well give thanks for editors.

Christ the Lord Is Risen Today

Wesley's "Hymn for Easter-Day" first appeared in the same 1739 collection. Another hymn of seven-syllable lines, it is almost as familiar as "Hark! The Herald Angels Sing." All our sample hymnals include the text (under "Christ the Lord Is Risen Today"). It has other similarities and has been as heavily cut, rearranged, and reassembled by compilers. The original lines, isolated by "alleluias," are something of a salad bar where we have picked and chosen what looked good.

Hymn for Easter-Day

1. "CHRIST the LORD is ris'n to Day,"
   Sons of Men and Angels say,
   Raise your Joys and Triumphs high,
   Sing ye Heav'ns, and Earth reply.

2. Love's Redeeming Work is done,
   Fought the Fight, the Battle won,
   Lo! our Sun's Eclipse is o'er,
   Lo! He sets in Blood no more.

3. Vain the Stone, the Watch, the Seal;
   CHRIST has burst the Gates of Hell!
   Death in vain forbids his Rise:
   CHRIST has open'd Paradise!

4. Lives again our glorious King,
   Where, O Death, is now thy Sting?
   Dying once he All doth save,
   Where thy Victory, O Grave?

5. Soar we now, where CHRIST has led?
   Following our Exalted Head,
   Made like Him, like Him we rise,
   Ours the Cross—the Grave—the Skies!

6. What tho' once we perish'd All,
   Partners in our Parent's Fall?
   Second Life we All receive,
   In our Heav'nly *Adam* live.

7. Ris'n with Him, we upward move,
   Still we seek the Things above,
   Still pursue, and kiss the Son
   Seated on his Father's Throne;

8. Scarce on Earth a Thought bestow,
   Dead to all we leave below,
   Heav'n our Aim, and lov'd Abode,
   Hid our Life with CHRIST in GOD!

9. Hid; till CHRIST our Life appear,
   Glorious in his Members here:
   Join'd to Him, we then shall shine
   All Immortal, all Divine!

10. Hail the LORD of Earth and Heav'n!
    Praise to Thee by both be giv'n:
    Thee we greet Triumphant now;
    Hail the Resurrection Thou!

11. King of Glory, Soul of Bliss,
    Everlasting Life is This,
    Thee to know, thy Pow'r to prove,
    Thus to sing, and thus to love!

We note several similarities to "Hark! The Herald Angels Sing": the seven-syllable lines are again assertive, beginning with a strong beat, reinforcing the series of commands; the lines are again paired in couplets by the pattern of rhyme; direct discourse, reminiscent of the angelic song of those herald angels, is once again moderately confusing; we find another visionary spectacle, signaled by *Lo!;* and, again, we "Hail" the Lord. The extensive cutting and pasting behind our modern versions also suggest a certain lack of control in the original.

The first stanza proceeds somewhat strangely: in the first line we announce the Resurrection, only to discover in the second line that this is part of the narrative, the story line of the hymn, the account of what people and angels are saying. Our forthright and unexceptionable proclamation is thus incorporated into an account, presumably our own, of an activity we are participating in. (But it's not that clear. The second line could also be a command, strangely following its carrying out: "Sons of men and Angels say, 'Christ the Lord. . . .'") In the third line somebody—not clearly identified as the singers, who have already both been proclaiming the Resurrection and reporting on what men and angels say or telling them to say what they have just said—is ordered to raise high joys and triumphs. In the final line it appears that the same somebody is telling the heavens to sing and the earth to reply. These fail to correlate nicely with earthlings and angels, however. We've all been singing the same proclamation together, and now, suddenly, this dialogue is suggested. Further problems include the missing article in the second line (common expression calls for "the angels"), the inappropriateness of *say* (rather than *exclaim, cry, shout*), and the obscurity of raising "triumphs." (The modern versions try to fix the second line—all but the Episcopalian, which wisely skips the first stanza altogether.)

We have seen how lines paired by rhymes encourage us to read these two-line pairs as units. Wesley tends to write single lines in isolation, each invoking powerful ideas but unrelated to the lines coming before or after. This tendency, along with the "alleluias," works against his chosen rhyme scheme. The punctuation introduced in the modern versions indicates an editorial attempt to insulate the incompatible ideas of each line from one another.

The second stanza divides more neatly into two couplets. The first stops commanding to report on the cause for joyful triumph—again, an odd reversal as one might think the cause should precede the effect. The cause for celebration is given using two metaphors, the completed *work* of redeeming Love and the *victory* in battle. Neither is explored or developed.

The tacit assumption seems to be either that the singers understand what these mean or that they don't need to.

We rush on to a vision, announced by *Lo!* (meaning "Look!"). It's a double vision, however, as the repeated *Lo!* suggests, and neither picture is clear. "Our Sun's Eclipse is o'er" brings together the familiar sun/Son pun with the darkening of the sky on Good Friday. The eclipse of the Sun is thus the death of Jesus. But what do we actually *see* when the eclipse of the Sun has passed? The hymn, it seems to me, owes us a clue. "Lo! He sets in Blood no more" is similarly problematical. The setting of the blood-red sun/Son on Calvary is one of the most powerful traditional pictures of Christian poetry. But what picture remains for us to look at when this image is, appropriately enough for a Resurrection hymn, canceled? Only the Lutherans retain the "Lo" lines. The other four hymnals in our sample skip to the second half of the next stanza, making one stanza of two.

As Wesley wrote it, the third stanza continues in the same fashion to attempt an account of the achievement of the Resurrection. The line-by-line fragmentation is again evident in the punctuation: the grammar fails to connect or relate the items. The "vain" uselessness of the stone, watch, and seal are only vaguely associated with the "vain" personification of Death of the third line and not at all connected to the gates of hell, except that they are similarly "burst." The picture of stones, watches, and seals is superseded rather than related to the more metaphorical "gates of hell." The activity of Christ's defiant bursting out (of grave and hell) is quickly replaced by the defiant rising motion, culminating in the opening of paradise, countering the closing of the tomb and of hell. The materials for a great stanza are all present, but they remain in something like draft form.

In the fourth stanza, retained in its entirety by all four modern hymnals, we try another tack. (The original stanza 4 becomes the Catholic stanza 2.) In the first couplet the opening assertion recalls the first line of the hymn and is followed by the taunt from Corinthians. (No matter that the personification of Death has only figured in this hymn as a vain forbidder of Christ's rising, not as a monster with a "sting." We're onto a new thought.) The second couplet almost defies analysis. "Dying once" is obscure. Do we mean "one time"? or "once upon a time"? or *once* that implies a "then"? Whichever meaning, some follow-through is called for, some explanation.

It is, however, not forthcoming. (To make matters worse, the *he* who died refers properly back to *death*, the most recent male noun.) While everybody has tried a repair, only the Presbyterians make much sense, with their "Jesus died, our souls to save." In the last line, the familiar challenge to the grave fails to recall, as it might have, the previous stanza, with its stone, watch, and seal. Too much has happened in the interim. The victory metaphor doesn't connect with the Fight and the Battle of the second stanza either. That was apparently another fight.

Modern editors have salvaged a stanza or two from the remaining seven (5–11), forcing order upon chaos. Episcopalians and Catholics conclude with the original stanza 5. Methodists fit it in as stanza 3. Everyone skips stanzas 6 through 9, however. Small wonder. A quick scanning of the long list of activities and topics shows how the hymn gets worse and worse. Wesley's tenth stanza becomes the new Lutheran and Methodist fifth stanza. The Presbyterians use its first two lines, invent a new conclusion, and call it quits. Indeed, here we note the same inversion that marred the first: we first hail the Lord and then call for such praise. In the second couplet we hail the Lord as the Resurrection—stirring but not too clear.

The final stanza (only the Lutherans and Methodists are still with us) provides reassurance that Wesley could sustain an idea through the course of a complete stanza—and it's a very good idea. To paraphrase, he has us say that to sing hymns, an act of witness and an expression of love, is to participate in everlasting life. In retrospect, pieces of the foregoing jumble fall into place. The idea of people singing together with angels, earth and heaven together, takes on new meaning. The images of the Resurrection, however fragmented, as portions of experience, have a purpose.

In both these hymns, "Hark! The Herald Angels" and "Christ the Lord Is Ris'n Today," Wesley's rush, his heaping on of ideas, may be excused as a kind of simulation of how our minds work when we are excited. His hymns may provoke an enthusiastic rush of response, a devotional high or "enthusiasm," to use the traditional term. The piling on of partial ideas raises the emotional pitch while it frustrates our demand for coherence. Perhaps the suspension of our demand for coherence is even the goal, the desired devotional end product. If this is so, we've come a long way from the hymns of Watts and their psalm models.

Oh, for a Thousand Tongues to Sing

This takes us naturally to the third of Wesley's hymns that we only sing in its heavily edited version. The hymn written "For the Anniversary Day of One's Conversion" was first published in 1740. It reflects the importance to the Methodists of a profound conversion experience, the kind of experience that we have seen transforming the hymn as we knew it. The text we know as "O for a Thousand Tongues" is extracted from this much longer work.

For the Anniversary Day of One's Conversion

1. Glory to GOD, and Praise, and Love
        Be ever, ever given;
    By Saints below, and Saints above,
        The Church in Earth and Heaven.

2. On this glad Day the glorious Sun
        Of Righteousness arose,
    On my benighted Soul he shone,
        And fill'd it with Repose.

3. Sudden expir'd the legal Strife,
        'Twas then I ceas'd to grieve,
    My Second, Real, Living Life
        I then began to live.

4. Then with my *Heart* I first believ'd,
        Believ'd, with Faith Divine,
    Power with the Holy Ghost receiv'd
        To call the Saviour *Mine*.

5. I felt my LORD's Atoning Blood
        Close to *my* Soul applied;
    Me, me he lov'd—the Son of GOD
        For *me,* for *me* He died!

6. I found, and own'd his Promise true,
   Ascertain'd of *my* Part,
   My Pardon pass'd in Heaven I *knew*
   When written on my Heart.

7. O for a Thousand Tongues to sing
   My dear Redeemer's Praise!
   The Glories of my GOD and King,
   The Triumphs of his Grace.

8. My gracious Master, and my GOD,
   Assist me to proclaim,
   To spread thro' all the Earth abroad
   The Honours of Thy Name.

9. JESUS the Name that charms our Fears,
   That bids our Sorrows cease;
   'Tis Musick in the Sinner's Ears,
   'Tis Life, and Health, and Peace!

10. He breaks the Power of cancell'd Sin,
    He sets the Prisoner free:
    His Blood can make the Foulest clean;
    His Blood avail'd for me.

11. He speaks; and listening to His Voice,
    New Life the Dead receive,
    The mournful, broken Hearts rejoice,
    The humble Poor *believe*.

12. Hear Him ye Deaf, His Praise ye Dumb
    Your loosen'd Tongues employ,
    Ye Blind, behold your Saviour come,
    And leap, ye Lame, for Joy.

13. Look unto Him, ye Nations, own
     Your GOD, ye fallen Race!
    Look, and be sav'd, thro' Faith alone;
     Be justified, by Grace!

14. See all your Sins on JESUS laid;
     The Lamb of GOD was slain,
    His Soul was once an Offering made
     For *every Soul* of Man.

15. Harlots, and Publicans, and Thieves
     In holy Triumph join!
    Sav'd is the Sinner that believes
     From Crimes as great as Mine.

16. Murtherers, and all ye hellish Crew,
     Ye Sons of Lust and Pride,
    Believe the Saviour died for you;
     For me the Saviour died.

17. Awake from guilty Nature's Sleep,
     And CHRIST shall give you Light,
    Cast all your Sins into the Deep,
     And wash the *Ethiop* white.

18. With me, your Chief, you then shall *know,*
     Shall feel your Sins forgiven;
    Anticipate your Heaven below,
     And own, that Love is Heaven.

We first observe that we're back to the common meter pattern of alternating lines of eight and six syllables and *abab* rhymes. We have commented that this form tends to be less assertive, less commanding, since each line normally begins with an unaccented syllable. We have also maintained that this form tightens the relationship among lines of a stanza, knitting them together with interlocking rhyme. Glancing down the right margin of this extraordinary hymn, note the relative absence of terminal punctuation (or *end-stopping,* to use the technical term) at the end of each line. This absence suggests that the ideas are regularly sustained past the single line unit.

Here, even more than with other texts, it is necessary to distinguish between the hymn Wesley wrote and the hymn we sing. The original is useful for what it tells us about the revival experience, hence the new kind of hymn we have been examining. The title assumes that every singer has had a profound, memorable, dateable conversion experience. The hymn act of commemorating that profoundly personal experience is part of revival devotion.

After the formal introductory "gloria" (which Lutherans and Episcopalians use as a finale and the other hymnals omit), the hymn begins with the image of the new day, the rising of the sun/Son and its illumination of the "benighted" soul. The effect is peace, or "repose." This unfortunately creates something of a metaphorical paradox, since the rising sun normally brings in a new day of work, not rest. The one exception is *Sun*day, the day of repose and the Resurrection, which suggests that the hymn makes sweet sense on condition that one's conversion happened on a Sunday. In the following stanza this "repose" becomes something more like peace, that which happens when the "strife" of the law suddenly dies—another item in Methodist conversion theology. Grieving ceases as suddenly, and the new life begins. As seen in stanza 4, this new life means a new kind of belief-with-the-heart and a new intimacy with the Lord as Savior. The profoundly personal nature of this experience is indicated in stanza 5, with its repetitions of *my* and *me.* Stanza 6 formulates the resulting conviction of salvation.

Nobody, however, sings stanzas 2 through 6 anymore. We all begin our versions with stanza 7. This wish for a thousand tongues can be taken in several ways. Most obviously, taken out of context, it is an imaginative expression of our inevitable inability to praise God adequately for all God's mercies: if I had a thousand tongues, I'd do better. This wish creates a monstrous picture, however (something like an illustration from a fairy tale about the misuse of wishes). The Thousand Tongues are, more reasonably and in the context of the hymn, rather the tongues of a thousand people, all praising "my" Redeemer. It is a wish for mass conversion, for revival. It recalls the glory and praises of the introductory stanza.

In the following stanza, we each ask for help with the task of proclamation, the task of the preacher as Christian witness. (The Presbyterians hold this stanza for their conclusion.) This is the call to revive, to awake the world—not, precisely, "the Earth." As we might expect in a hymn so grounded in the writer's personal life—albeit available for congregational generalization—the dominant picture is that of a preacher, praying publicly for assistance before beginning a rousing sermon. While common folk lead lives of Christian witness, we don't quite do so "thro' all the Earth abroad." The message is not, precisely, that of salvation, but rather the less direct "Honours of Thy Name," to be enumerated in the following stanza.

The Lutheran alteration of "Jesus the Name" to "The name of Jesus" was a good idea. In both the original and the other modern versions, the accent on the second syllable, demanded by the metrical pattern of stresses, unfortunately distorts the very name which is to be celebrated. No such simple editing can or has attempted to correct the subsequent faults of the stanza, however, the familiar problems of unassimilated ideas. That the name of Jesus "charms our Fears" at first may strike us as bizarre. We are more familiar with the modern idea of charming as alluring or delighting—the name of Jesus certainly doesn't do that to our fears. Of course, Wesley meant *charms* in another sense, that which, sung or chanted, magically controls. The name has incantatory power over our anxieties.

Although this idea of "charming" could use some explanation, we rush on to another vague activity of the name, its bidding. Indeed, how can a "name" bid our "Sorrows cease"? Jesus might, or we might, but I am at a loss to explain logically how the name can do this. Nor does Wesley stop to clarify. He hastens on to his new metaphors: the first of these identifies the name as "Musick in the Sinner's Ears." This recalls the idea of the name as charming fears, but not very precisely—charming fears and music in the ears don't lock together meaningfully. It also implies that the music of the hymn itself, the music the congregation is engaged in, is somehow—albeit vaguely—related to that name and its power. The three heavyweight metaphors of the last line are no more integrated. *How* is the name "Life, and Health, and Peace"? Or, alternatively, *how* does the name "bring" these things?

The next stanza—wisely deleted by the Episcopalians and heavily modified by the Presbyterians—fails to explain, shifting us from the sketchy review of the achievements of the name to Jesus himself, where we encounter new difficulties. "He breaks the Power of cancell'd Sin" is problematic. The "power of Sin" introduces the idea of an important power struggle between a heroic Jesus and the personification of Sin, the seed of a good idea. To "break the Power of *cancell'd* Sin" is, however, simply pointless. If sin is already canceled, breaking its power is unnecessary. (The Presbyterian "*reigning* Sin" improves things.) In Wesley's original, we don't explore what's left of the idea, but turn rather to the liberation of "the Prisoner." Jesus as liberator is another important germ of an idea, grounded in tradition, which doesn't work here. Jesus may free those unjustly imprisoned or free us from the metaphorical prison of fear and sin and damnation, but this simple, unexplained liberation of "the prisoner" is troubling, even subversive. (Here the Presbyterian alteration, "Christ's Blood can make the sinful clean" seems sadly mistaken as it keeps the cleansing metaphor but deletes the foul need.)

We rush on to a new idea, the idea of cleansing blood. A speedy personal testimony follows: "His Blood avail'd for me." We recall the revival, the primacy of conversion and public testimonial, the context of the larger hymn as an anniversary celebration, which the sometime modern change to the present-tense *avails* attempts to disguise. Disguised, however, the line means little.

Only the Episcopalians and the Methodists retain stanzas 11 and 12. Then they quit, too. Given the length and disorder of the hymn, the modern elimination of stanzas is certainly understandable. We note the rhetorical patterning, however, which shapes the hymn and which all but the Methodist editors have missed: as stanza 10 began with "He breaks," stanza 11 opens with "He speaks" and proceeds to explain the new life and general rejoicing that had been introduced and left dangling at the end of stanza 9. Stanza 12, with its deaf and dumb and blind audience, dramatizes the "health" of that last line of stanza 9. Stanzas 13 and 14 explain the deliverance celebrated back in stanza 10. Stanzas 15 and 16 expatiate on the foulest who need cleaning, also in stanza 10. Stanza 18 refers the whole progress of the hymn to the account of the conversion of St. Paul, justifying and shaping it retrospectively. Only the Methodists retain this final word.

IV: The Best of Wesley

Charles Wesley also wrote more coherent hymns, and, with great pleasure, we turn to examine three of these. The three examples of Wesley at his best all show him using alternating lines of eight and seven syllables, knit together with alternating rhymes. The thought is clear and the hymns progress logically. They have not had to be substantially changed by editors.

Come, Thou Long-Expected Jesus

"Dear Desire of Every Nation" ("Come, Thou Long-Expected Jesus"), first published in the *Nativity Hymns* of 1745, is a collective prayer. The first-person singular pronoun is notably absent:

Dear Desire of Every Nation

1. Come Thou long-expected JESUS,
    Born to set thy people free,

From our Fears and Sins relieve us,
  Let us find our Rest in Thee:
Israel's Strength and Consolation,
  Hope of all the Earth Thou art,
Dear Desire of every Nation,
  Joy of every longing Heart.

2. Born thy People to deliver,
      Born a Child and yet a King,
    Born to reign in Us for ever,
      Now thy gracious Kingdom bring;
    By thine own eternal Spirit
      Rule in all our Hearts alone,
    By thine all-sufficient Merit
      Raise us to thy glorious Throne.

The original punctuation—the colon and semicolon—indicates that the two long stanzas divide neatly into four units of four lines each, a subdivision that becomes useful as we track the progression of ideas. (The hymn can be sung in both two-stanza and four-stanza versions.)

The first two lines establish the collective voice and the main idea of the hymn, a voice and an idea that Wesley successfully maintains throughout the text. Here *we* address Jesus, consistently and without exception. We ask him to *come* for a variety of reasons which are carefully explicated and interrelated in the lines that follow. Our long *expectation* of Jesus, his role as *liberator,* and his role as *king* are all explained. The hymn, in short, returns us to the Watts model of a text that teaches as it articulates proper devotional attitudes in poetic language that is at once succinct and evocative.

In the third line, the alteration—by all five modern hymnals—of *relieve* to *release* deserves comment. The change of the metaphor to "release" is based on the assumption that Wesley is explaining the *freedom* Jesus is born to bring (line 2) as *release* from fears and sins. The new semicolon, replacing a comma, at the end of the line further associates the fears and sins with the freeing action of line 2. In the original, where we pray for *relief* from fears and sins, this relieving action introduces the "Rest" we want to find in "Thee," the subject of the following line. The idea of rest is, with the alteration, cut off and appears tagged on. In fact the idea of "Let us find our Rest in Thee" is a noble pun, best known in the poem "The Pulley" by the seventeenth-century poet George Herbert. To "find our Rest" is at once to find repose or respite or relief from stress, a place to stop, and, at the same time, our remainder or balance. Only the GIA editors understood and altered the fourth line to read "Free us from captivity." The elimination of "Rest" is at least completed, the corpse removed.

In all but the GIA version, what we find "in Thee" is witnessed by "thy people" through time and across space, from Old Testament times to the present, from the nations to the individual heart. (All this may be read as an explanation of "long-expected" in the first line. These are the people who have long expected Jesus.) Wesley's account, in lines 5 through 8, sweeps from the "Strength and Consolation" of Israel (compare "our fears and sins" which require strength and consolation) in the past to the wide-angle lens of the "Hope of all the Earth" (compare "expected," which looks to hope) across space. In the last two lines, the sweep moves from the breadth of "every Nation" to the fine focused intimacy "of every longing Heart." Our "rest" has been, in lines 5 through 8, defined as strength, consolation, dearly desired hope, and heart's joy. (The GIA alterations of lines 6 and 8 are consistent.)

The second stanza elegantly reworks and clarifies the ideas of the first. In the first three hymns we considered, Wesley's rhetorical patterns often prepared us for a kind of incantatory incoherence, and his lists of images failed to lead anywhere. Here we find something else entirely. The rhetorical repetition signals an itemization, shaped and directed.

We have read the second half of the first stanza as a commentary explaining the first line of the stanza, explaining the expectation and what it signified, in the past and present. Similarly, the first three lines of the second stanza, each beginning with *Born*, explain and detail the second line of the first stanza, "Born to set thy people free." "Born thy People to deliver" is a simple paraphrase, recalling line 2 to us (perhaps reminding us of how "thy People" has been glossed in lines 5 through 8 to include Israel, all the Earth, every Nation, and every longing Heart.) "Born . . . to deliver" also suggests delivery as birth, that Jesus was born to supervise our new birth as his people. The second line, "Born a Child and yet a King," concisely juxtaposes the fact of infancy with the regal birth, the point of countless paintings and sculptures of the regal baby. The third line explains this royalty over us—"for ever." The initial *Now* of the next line, following *for ever,* emphasizes the immediacy of the prayer that Jesus "Come." *Bring* is the concluding command of this half stanza, balancing that initial *come.*

The last four lines assimilate the ideas of the preceding twelve. Two new petitions, "rule" and "raise," are added to the series that have shaped the lines (Come . . . relieve . . . bring . . .). We have been, through the hymn, working on ideas of kingship, reigning, and kingdoms, so that the prayer that Jesus "Rule in all our Hearts alone," by means of the Spirit, makes good sense. We have been contemplating broadly political power as well as the joy of the longing heart. The juxtaposition of eternity and the private world comes clear: the messianic achievement and the royal domination are at once public and private.

The last two lines, the final petition that we be raised to glory, seem at first reading to be off on another tack, a typical Wesleyan digression. Why are we suddenly singing about our *elevation* to the throne of Jesus in a basic liberation hymn? The answer, I think, takes us back to the third line of the first stanza, "From our Fears and Sins relieve us." The petition demonstrates the important double action of the hymn: the desired freedom is both horizontal-political-psychological release and a vertical springing free, an unburdening relief from oppression. Looking back, the first four lines of the second stanza dramatize this turning to the vertical axis. The birth of the King, emphasized in the repetitions, and his power over us culminate perfectly in our own, unmerited but reciprocal, elevation.

Indeed, looking back at the four half stanzas of this hymn, we find a remarkably intricate pattern. The first two articulate and explain anticipation through time and space. They are grounded in the experience of the faithful. They are horizontal, linear. The first stresses *activities* desired—coming, freeing, relieving, finding rest. The second *details the subject,* that is coming—as strength and consolation, hope, desire, joy. (The verb form *thou art* is a sign that this is what's going on.) The second pair of half stanzas switches gracefully to the transcendental, vertical achievement of the coming, the fact of and meaning of the coming of the Kingdom with the birth of a Child-King.

The reign, achieved, moves us onto another axis, which explains the balance of ruling (downward) and raising (upward). The suggestion of rising implicit in our being relieved of fear and sin, back in the experientially grounded first stanza, can only happen, only spring free, through the birth and the rule, explained in the intervening lines. If Wesley had left us with rule only, the result would have been a metaphor of oppressive domination. We must, in the end, be raised to glory, to the height of that throne.

Love Divine, All Loves Excelling

"Love Divine, All Loves Excelling," first published in the *Redemption Hymns* of 1747, is Charles Wesley's most famous hymn celebration of divine love. Like "Come, Thou Long-Expected Jesus," the text alternates eight- and seven-syllable lines, interlocked with rhyme—which, as it encourages sustained thought, is generally Wesley's most successful meter. Like the former hymn, it is a prayer sung in a collective voice. Its modern acceptability is evident in the paucity of modern alterations and the relative absence of cuts. (The Episcopalians and the Catholics excise stanza 2.)

Love Divine, All Loves Excelling

1. Love Divine, all Loves excelling,
        Joy of Heaven to Earth come down,
    Fix in us thy humble Dwelling,
        All thy faithful Mercies crown;
    JESU, Thou art all Compassion,
        Pure unbounded Love Thou art,
    Visit us with thy Salvation,
        Enter every trembling Heart.

2. Breathe, Oh breathe thy loving Spirit
        Into every troubled Breast,

Let us all in Thee inherit,
 Let us find that Second Rest:
Take away our Power of sinning,
 Alpha and Omega be,
End of Faith as its Beginning,
 Set our Hearts at Liberty.

3. Come, Almighty to deliver,
 Let us all thy Life receive,
Suddenly return, and never,
 Never more thy Temples leave.
Thee we would be always blessing,
 Serve Thee as thy Hosts above.
Pray, and praise Thee without ceasing,
 Glory in thy perfect Love.

4. Finish then thy New Creation,
 Pure and sinless let us be,
Let us see thy great Salvation,
 Perfectly restor'd in Thee;
Chang'd from Glory into Glory,
 Till in Heaven we take our Place,
Till we cast our Crowns before Thee,
 Lost in Wonder, Love, and Praise.

Wesley's first verse is unexceptionable, coherent—and rich enough to turn us back to our dictionary. Our appreciation only increases when we examine details of the poetic expression. In the first line, for example, the phrase "all Loves excelling" at first only means that God's love is better than mortal loves—a fine idea, although nothing extraordinary. New possibilities of meaning open up when we realize that plural *loves,* to Wesley and his contemporaries, were not just the abstraction or particular mortal attachments but also *amores,* the little winged cupids of valentine cards, carrying the arrows of sexual desire. The amores are at once diminutive, even comical, and quasi-divine. The original strength of the verb *to excel* remains in our word *excellence*—"to surpass others especially in good qualities, laudable actions, or acquirements." Divine love may thus be explained with reference to the little amores, but takes us far beyond and above these common poetical children.

If the first line refers to the transcendent "Love Divine" by means of common loves, the second line covers the same distance, moving in the opposite direction. (This is the task, it seems, of divine love hymnody, this negotiation of the distance between the Lover and object.) Divine love as the "Joy of Heaven" is richly suggestive: Jesus Christ is the Joy of Heaven come down; Love is joy; heavenly joy is, almost by definition, unattainable on earth, hence miraculously "come down." Further, readjusting the emphases, we hear that the joy proceeds from the phenomenon of "Heaven to Earth come down." Just below the surface of all these suggestions lies the ancient cosmic sexual image of the divine marriage of Heaven and Earth, their joy and fecund love.

Such downcoming leads naturally to the domesticity of the third line: Love Divine is to inhabit the "humble Dwelling" of each human heart. To *fix* is, variously, to secure, to settle, "to give definite, visible, or fixed form to (something that is intangible, fleeting, or elusive)," and, of course, to "repair." The Dwelling is "humble" because we are conscious of our contemptible condition in contrast to God's glory and "thy humble" Dwelling because of the willing humility of the divine Lover. This love as the "crown" of "all thy faithful mercies" balances the humility: the willing downcoming of Jesus, in love, his residence here, "crowns" us, raises us up.

The second half of the first stanza explicitly identifies Jesus as that Love Divine which has been carefully explicated in the first four lines. With the naming of Jesus, and, by implication, through the Incarnation, we sing of a new kind of love, compassionate and saving, subtly distinct, however related to the humble descent of love from heaven to earth, illustrated and dramatized above. *Compassion* suggests mutuality, love of fellow beings, a lateral love. The image of "unbounded Love" continues on this horizontal metaphorical axis. This love culminates in another "visitation"—not quite the Divine Lover, knocking at the door, which would have fit with the language of the first four lines, but rather the archaic meaning of *visit* "to come to or upon as a spiritual help" or comfort, befitting Jesu as "all

Compassion." The entrance into "every trembling Heart" provides saving comfort rather than the ecstatic gratification which is the divine love norm.

Stepping back from the first stanza, we see how words and images from the first and second halves are juxtaposed:

(lines 1–4)	*(lines 5–8)*
Love Divine	Jesu
cupids	compassion
to excel	fellow-feeling
joy come down	unbounded
fix	visit
humble dwelling	salvation
crown	enter
mercies	trembling heart

The second half of the stanza counters the traditional divine love picture with a more "modern" and humanitarian idea of divine lovingkindness, sympathetic and reassuring. (The Catholics have chosen to resist this humanitarian shift in language. Instead of Jesus *as* all Compassion, he is its *source,* which remains vertical, disembodied. In the following line, the GIA text substitutes "Love unbounded, love all pure"—of which Jesus is, presumably, still the *source.* When the last line becomes "Let your love in us endure," it is still a general rather than a specific idea.)

The second stanza proceeds in this same direction, losing the Episcopalians and the Catholics along the way. It begins with a prayer for something of a kiss: "Breathe, O breathe thy loving Spirit / Into every troubled Breast" belongs to the divine love convention—and summons the lovely old idea of kisses as "animate," as the exchange of vital spirit or breath. But these kisses, this breathing, is meant to soothe "every troubled Breast," recalling the visitation of "every trembling Heart" at the end of the prior stanza. Their function is calming, as becomes apparent in the third and fourth lines, where what we want is rest, the cessation of trembling and troubles. (The primary meaning of "inheriting" such rest is simple possession or receiving. The subtle suggestion of our inheritance as heirs— siblings of Christ and children of God—is not reinforced by any other imagery. Note also the unfortunate isolation of the third line by the new Lutheran and Methodist semicolons preceding and following it.)

This "Second Rest," the suspension of the will, is the desired goal. (Lutherans and Presbyterians substitute "promised rest.") So the original reads "Take away our Power of sinning," an idea displeasing to editors, who have substituted "Take away the love of sinning" or "our bent to sinning." We may presume that the implied loss of free will worried the editors, who couldn't wait for freedom until the end of the stanza. The substitute lines attempt to obscure the ecstatic passivity that lies at the heart of the hymn. The one version also injects another love (that of sinning), which has no real role to play in the unfolding drama. In fact the divine confiscation of ("take away") our *power* of sinning is inseparable—as suggested by the original punctuation—from the absolute everythingness of God, Alpha and Omega. It is our recognition, by grace and the breathing of "thy loving Spirit," of God as the Alpha and the Omega that both "takes away our *power* of sinning" and "Sets our hearts at Liberty."

Wesley's second stanza is, admittedly, a bit difficult to follow. The key is in precise tracking of lines 6 and 7, the theological bridge between our confiscated power of sinning and our liberation.

Alpha and Omega be,
End of Faith as its Beginning . . .

These two lines belong together, linked by the verb *be* and the grammatical structure of apposition. Love Divine, as Jesus, whom we address throughout this hymn, is identified as Alpha and Omega, the totality *of faith,* its beginning and end. This is elegantly done. The normal appositive structure would be Alpha and Omega, Beginning and End (i.e., Alpha is to Beginning as Omega is to End). By inverting the order, we end up back where we began: Alpha . . . Omega . . . End . . . Beginning—caught up in a circle without beginning or end.

The two lines should *never* be separated by a semicolon, a crime committed by the editors of all four hymnals. The semicolon gives us "Alpha and Omega be" as an absurd independent command. What can it possibly mean to tell Jesus Christ, whom we confess *is,* to *be* Alpha and

Omega? And what happens to the next line, stripped of its verb? (Indeed, the major problem with the second stanza as we have it is not theological but editorial, especially the fragmentation of the ideas resulting from heavy-handed punctuation. Note how commas become semicolons and the colon becomes a period.)

The liberty of our hearts that proceeds from such a faith, breathed into us by the Spirit, beginning and ending in the Lord, is explained in the third stanza. Love Divine, as Jesus, whom we address throughout, is petitioned to "Come" as one "Almighty to deliver," i.e., having the power to deliver. The Lutheran introduction of a comma after *Almighty* breeds unspeakable confusion, suggesting that the first person of the Trinity, rather than Jesus, is suddenly addressed. Jesus has sufficient power; we pray we might receive all *his* Life in the next line—not the life of the "Almighty." Such life-receiving recalls the breathing of the loving Spirit in the preceding stanza as well as our inheritance of Rest. Love delivers us, frees us, as it gives us life.

Beginning with the third stanza, the conventional eagerness of divine love, bred of frustrated imaginings, takes over. We have commended Love Divine, described its descent, begged for its entrance. We have examined compassionate love, comforting love, the transformation of life through faith. We proceed to the urgent petition for immediate action. From this angle, "Let us all thy Life receive" suggests the incompleteness of redemption until the Coming of the Lord, "suddenly" and forever. Our strong desire to join the heavenly hosts ("Thee we would be always blessing"— the GIA alteration undermines the grammar) is a desire for human action, action entirely missing from the first eighteen lines of the hymn, which have petitioned or described activity of the Lord. The Coming frees us to, as it gives us Life for, the blessing, serving, praying, praising without ceasing, and glorying which follow. While a certain poignancy adheres to this activity which we "would be" pursuing if the Lord would only return, the structure also expresses simple will to worship, presumably shared by all singers.

As is so often the case with Charles Wesley's hymns, the last stanza provides a *re*-vision of the preceding lines. Here the revision proceeds from the direct invocation of Revelation 21:1–7:

And I saw a new heaven and a new earth: for the first heaven and the first earth were passed away; and there was no more sea. And I John saw the holy city, new Jerusalem, coming down from God out of heaven, prepared as a bride adorned for her husband. And I heard a great voice out of heaven saying, Behold, the tabernacle of God is with men, and he will dwell with them, and they shall be his people, and God himself will be with them and be their God. And God shall wipe away all tears from their eyes; and there shall be no more death, neither sorrow, nor crying, neither shall there be any more pain: for the former things are passed away!

And he that sat up on the throne said, Behold, I make all things new! . . . I am Alpha and Omega, the beginning and the end. I will give unto him that is athirst of the fountain of the water of life freely. He that overcometh shall inherit all things; and I will be his God, and he shall be my son. *(Authorized Version / King James)*

We see where Wesley found his New Creation, the new order to come, celebrated in the final stanza. We also recognize the Beloved, coming out of heaven like a bride, Christ dwelling among men, the compassion and the end to troubles, the Alpha and Omega, the inheritance. The pieces fall into place.

Wesley has eased us into Revelation. The prayed-for deliverance is one with the completion of the New Creation. The prayed-for seizure of our power of sinning is one with our purity and sinlessness in the new order. The private visitation by salvation of the first stanza has become the public, visible "great Salvation" of the ultimate, restored worship in heaven.

Lo! He Comes with Clouds Descending

Our final sample of Wesleyan hymnody, "Lo! He Comes with Clouds Descending," included in all but the Catholic collection, is also based on Revelation:

> Behold, he is coming with the clouds! Every eye shall see
> him, and among them those who pierced him; and all
> the peoples of the world shall lament in remorse. So it
> shall be. Amen. (1:7)

First published as "Thy Kingdom Come!" in the *Hymns of Intercession for
all Mankind* (1758), the hymn is accordingly visionary. Note how each
stanza is also tightly bound by rhymes.

Thy Kingdom Come!

1. Lo! He comes with clouds discending,
    Once for favour'd sinners slain!
    Thousand, thousand saints attending,
    Swell the triumph of his train:
    Hallelujah,
    GOD appears, on earth to reign!

2. Every eye shall now behold Him
    Rob'd in dreadful majesty,
    Those who set at nought and sold Him,
    Pierc'd, and nail'd Him to the tree,
    Deeply wailing
    Shall the true Messiah see.

3. The dear tokens of his passion
    Still his dazling body bears,
    Cause of endless exultation
    To his ransom'd worshippers;
    With what rapture
    Gaze we on those glorious scars!

4. Yea, amen! let all adore Thee
    High on thine eternal throne

Saviour, take the power and glory
Claim the kingdom for thine own:
JAH, JEHOVAH,
Everlasting GOD, come down

As usual, *Lo!* signals a spectacle, conjured for our delight. Here as in Revelation, we envision the Second Coming. As in the final stanza of "Love Divine," this is somewhat touching, an imaginative exercise in hope. (Wishing, however spectacular, can't make it happen.)

The first stanza presents a triangular tableau, literally spilling out of heaven. The figure of the Lord, at the lowest point of the triangle, is attended by the sort of clouds that figure in countless Baroque altar-paintings, all involved in the "train" of thousands of saints. "God appears on earth to reign" suggests a glorious earth landing. Such an appearance, we have learned, often has certain fertility associations and both the clouds and the familiar rain/reign pun call up those associations. Through the visionary mechanism, the future becomes present and the main verbs are in the present tense: "He comes" and the "saints . . . swell" and "God appears." The royalty of the glorified Christ heightens the language and enhances the spectacle. That we are "favour'd" sinners suggests royal favor, as does the immense retinue, the "triumph" and the "train." Royal personages make "appearances."[*]

The vision involves us, as singers, both by the imaginative power whereby we see what isn't there, and by including us in the action. This is participatory theater. We sing along with the "thousand, thousand saints" and "Swell the triumph of his train" with our repeated "Hallelujahs."

As we join the train, the camera angle shifts—in cinematic fashion—from the spectacle itself to the lifted eyes of the spectators. A new triangle emerges, the broad base on earth, the focal point—the Cross—raised. The robes of dreadful majesty, a broad-based triangle, reinforce this new geometry. Among the spectators are the guilty, with whom we identify when we

---

[*] The Presbyterian substitution of "See the Lamb for sinners slain!" for Wesley's line 2 ruins the spectacle. The Lamb doesn't fit; the hymn isn't about lambs. Similarly, the substitution of "Join to sing the glad refrain" for the fourth line confuses the triangular geometry.

"wail deeply" over and over again, just as we sang Hallelujahs with the saints in the preceding stanza. Just as the "dreadful Majesty" was anticipated with the royal language of the first stanza, so the triumphant body of the following stanza is anticipated here. (The Presbyterian shift of the beholding action from now to then goes against the presentness of the whole hymn. The change in address—the Presbyterian version has us speak to the Lord—is premature.)

The third stanza closes in at shorter range on the "dear tokens" borne by the "dazling body." "Tokens" are an interesting choice of image for Christ's wounds, suggesting signs and proofs, marks, emblems, pledges and, most remarkably, coins. As signs and proofs they are "dear" in the sense of "beloved." As pledges and coins they are "dear" in the sense of "precious" or "costly." This financial idea is confirmed by the image of "ransom'd worshippers," ransomed by the wounds as tokens as coin. We recall the poor values of the guilty, who "set him at nought" and "sold him," how they undervalued the coin. In contrast, these worshipers in the third stanza, among whom we count ourselves, are enraptured at the sight of the tokens. As usual, rapture causes Wesley to abandon coherence, and he has us both exulting endlessly, presumably making an incessant noise, and gazing in rapture, a presumably silent activity. (Presbyterians don't sing this stanza.)

The fourth stanza is different. In what went before, we have swept from heaven to earth, from the Hallelujahs of the saints to the wailing of the sinners. The present tense has tricked us with its visionary force into pretending to see what hasn't yet happened and pretending to participate in the final coming of the kingdom. The fourth stanza restores us to the present—a flashback to reality. The rapture of adoration is sustained, but the Saviour is back in heaven, "High on thine eternal throne." Now we command universal worship ("let all adore thee") and pray for those events we have been imaginatively foreseeing ("take . . . Claim . . . come"). However intricate, the narrative strategy is successful.

A final note on the editing of this hymn is in order. Indeed, the whole has been subtly changed by all the hymnals but the Methodist to substitute cautious Christocentrism for Wesley's careful monotheism. At the end of the first stanza, where Wesley had "God appears, on earth to reign!" we find

"Christ the Lord returns to reign." In the final stanza, everyone modifies the praise for Jehovah to the repeated "Alleluias." In the last line "Everlasting God, come down" is replaced with "Thou shalt reign, and thou alone" (or the Presbyterian "Everlasting Christ, come down"), clearly referring to the Saviour of line 3. The editorial changes seem designed to keep singers from confusing the persons of the Trinity. They cost the hymn dearly, however, obscuring Wesley's fine point that Christ the Lord is God made manifest, who, in the final Revelation, will be revealed as "Everlasting God, come down."

V: The Olney Hymns

A sampling of the *Olney Hymns,* written by John Newton (1725–1807) and William Cowper (1731–1800) and published in 1779, concludes our survey of eighteenth-century hymnody. Because "Amazing Grace" has achieved the modern status of popular song, it offers special lessons in what hymns are and how they work. No less accessible, "The Name of Jesus" treats metaphor, ever a central concern of Christian poets and readers. "Zion, or the City of God" provides yet another lively biblical tableau. While Newton's hymns encourage discussion of popular appeal and hymn method, William Cowper's contributions to the collection force consideration of private vision and the hymn writer as poet.

Amazing Grace, How Sweet the Sound

Newton's "Amazing Grace," even more than Watts's "Joy to the World," reminds us of the contemporary liveliness of certain eighteenth-century poems. Loved by congregations, this hymn, sung to the tune New Britain from *Virginia Harmony,* is a staple of country, folk, and gospel recording. Newton's original title, "Faith's Review and Expectation," referred readers to 1 Chronicles 17:16, 17.

Faith's Review and Expectation

1. Amazing grace! (how sweet the sound!)
   That sav'd a wretch like me!
   I once was lost, but now am found,
   Was blind, but now I see.

2. 'Twas grace that taught my heart to fear,
   And grace my fears reliev'd;
   How precious did that grace appear,
   The hour I first believ'd!

3. Thro' many dangers, toils, and snares,
   I have already come;
   'Tis grace has brought me safe thus far,
   And grace will lead me home.

4. The Lord has promis'd good to me,
   His word my hope secures;
   He will my shield and portion be
   As long as life endures.

5. Yea, when this flesh and heart shall fail,
   And mortal life shall cease;
   I shall possess, within the vail,
   A life of joy and peace.

6. The earth shall soon dissolve like snow,
   The sun forbear to shine;
   But God, who call'd me here below,
   Will be for ever mine.

These words are so familiar, so seemingly simple, that we bring out our bag of critical tools with a nervous smile, worried about pedantry. The memory of the strengths hidden in "Joy to the World," and, perhaps, the hidden weaknesses of "Hark! The Herald Angels," reinforce our resolve.

As usual, the original title, unavailable in our modern hymnals, provides useful direction to our reading: the hymn will look back in time, tracing the experience of faith (i.e., "review"), and forward, anticipating the future (i.e., "expectation"). The hymn voice is very simple: "I," a sinner, give public testimony to my state. Neither praise nor prayer is offered, but rather a simple, universal confessional formula, the history of any believer, told to anyone who will listen. The "I" is thus "exemplary," a role for every man and woman to assume and to assimilate.

The stanza begins in wonder, with an exclamation that can mean many things. We might exclaim at the "Amazing grace" of an athlete or a dancer. Or "Grace" might be an amazing woman. (The original exclamation point, as it isolates the exclamation, encourages such reflection.) Grace is also, of course, a doctrine, a gift, and a state that proceed from God. As such, grace is amazing in a more radical and powerful sense, causing wonder and bewilderment. The second half of the first line belongs in its original parentheses, a comment or aside on the exclamation. When the words *how sweet the sound* are instead put between commas, they introduce the confusing suggestion that the "sweet sound," rather than grace itself, saved me (i.e., "the sound, that saved . . . "). All our hymnals perpetuate this confusion.

The second line tells us that "Amazing grace," whatever it is, is known, firsthand, as efficacious. The state of "wretchedness" is the opposite of grace. A *wretch* is an outcast, sunk in degradation, criminal, foul, despicable. Our experience of salvation—both in life and in this hymn—is what teaches us what grace is and how it is amazing. The condition of wretchedness, now past, is described in exquisitely simple terms of being lost and being blind, primal terms accessible to every human soul. (Newton's own dramatic life experience and the miserable conditions of his parishioners at Olney provide touching biographical and historical context of the sort we have sworn to avoid as unnecessary and distracting.) The parables and miracles of Jesus are involved as well, the lost sheep and the blind restored to sight. Of course, these are basic metaphors, allowing the experience of grace to be described with reference to familiar physical conditions. Such wretchedness is also in sharp contrast to the secular suggestions of *grace* as sweet, charming, agile, sure-footed.

We don't *need* to identify these allusions to parables and miracles to understand the simple meaning of the hymn. When we see how rich the associations are, however, the power of the parables and miracles attaches itself to our experience of the hymn, enhancing it. This is especially the case with the third line, "I once was lost, but now am found," which echoes exactly the Father's joy at the recovery of his Prodigal Son. Indeed, our identification with the "wretch" takes us naturally to that parable.

The second stanza explains the working of grace, the process of conversion, assignable to a definite hour. (Newton was a Calvinist Evangelical within the Anglican tradition.) With the picture of grace as a teacher ("'Twas grace that taught my heart to fear") we recall the initial suggestion of "Amazing grace" as a woman named Grace. A particularly lively personification, in the next line she gives kindly comfort ("And grace my fears relieved"). The following lines change metaphors and give us grace as a treasure, the value of which becomes apparent only at conversion.

The third stanza continues "Faith's Review" of past experience. The first stanza had recalled the passive "wretchedness" and "lostness" and "blindness" of life before salvation. The third stanza describes an active mortal life of "dangers, toils, and snares," adventures to be negotiated. The difference in perspective is significant. Since the first stanza we have acknowledged the conversion which transforms a life of passive, wretched oppression to one of active sainthood. Saints take the evils of life in stride, led toward home by grace. In this stanza, the personification of grace is a protector and guide, recalling the mentors, male and female, of epics, those traditional adventure stories, or perhaps even Obi Wan Kenobi from *Star Wars.*

The confidence in that homecoming, based on experience of grace, marks the turning point, here at the middle of the original six-stanza hymn, from "Faith's Review" to "Expectation." "The Lord" is now the subject, replacing "Grace." The Prodigal, led home by grace, is received by the Lord. His word is the guarantee of that hope born of experience of grace.

In the second half of this stanza, the Lord as "shield" would seem to take the place of grace as "guide" in the preceding stanza. The Lord as "portion" yet again calls the Prodigal Son to mind, his original request for his portion (as in the *King James Version*), and his final, richer portion. (When the Episcopalians and Catholics reverse stanzas 3 and 4, they oversimplify the action of the hymn and misplace the Prodigal idea.)

The last two stanzas of the original hymn projected this expectation into the future, to death, the afterlife, on past the end of the world. Perhaps their confidence mitigates the tendency of Christians to rest on their earthly attainment of salvation. Death is confronted graphically and the afterlife proclaimed. The cataclysm is expected and confidently transcended. Only the Methodists sing stanza 5. Nobody includes stanza 6. If we see this life of faith as eternal, we miss the last two stanzas.[*]

How Sweet the Name of Jesus Sounds

While equally accessible to the uncritical singer, Newton's hymn on "The Name of Jesus" ("How Sweet the Name of Jesus Sounds") is, as the original title suggests, a virtual study in metaphorical theology. (Methodists and Presbyterians have not included it.) The "name" is powerful:

The Name of Jesus

1. How sweet the name of Jesus sounds
    In a believer's ear!
    It soothes his sorrows, heals his wounds,
    And drives away his fear.

---

[*] All the modern hymnals, excepting the Lutherans, replace the last two stanzas with a new conclusion, credited by two to John Res. The lines are as follows:

> When we've been there ten thousand years,
> bright shining as the sun,
> we've no less days to sing God's praise
> than when we first begun.

If our reading of Newton's original is at all accurate, this appended stanza is oddly inappropriate. Why the leap into eternity? How does this riddle fit with the message of the hymn?

2. It makes the wounded spirit whole,
   And calms the troubled breast;
   'Tis manna to the hungry soul,
   And to the weary rest.

3. Dear name! the rock on which I build,
   My shield and hiding-place;
   My never-failing treas'ry, fill'd
   With boundless stores of grace.

4. By thee my pray'rs acceptance gain,
   Altho' with sin defil'd;
   Satan accuses me in vain,
   And I am own'd a child.

5. JESUS! my Shepherd, Husband, Friend,
   My Prophet, Priest, and King!
   My Lord, my Life, my Way, my End!
   Accept the praise I bring.

6. Weak is the effort of my heart,
   And cold my warmest thought;
   But when I see thee as thou art,
   I'll praise thee as I ought.

7. Till then I would thy love proclaim
   With ev'ry fleeting breath;
   And may the music of thy name
   Refresh my soul in death.

The "sweetness" of the name is romantic, and Newton's headnote makes explicit reference to the Song of Songs: "Your love is more fragrant than wine, fragrant is the scent of your perfume, and your name like perfume poured out; for this the maidens love you" (1:2–3). Sweetness—like the sweet sound of "Amazing grace"—suggests scent and taste, as well as hearing sweet music and loving sentiment. (The Catholic substitution of "How *good*" is timid, even ascetic.) Newton defers romance, however, in the interest of childhood experience. In the first two stanzas of "The Name of Jesus," the sweet name of Jesus is illustrated in a remarkable series of verb metaphors, all nurturant, maternal, soothing. As the name soothes sorrows, heals wounds, drives away fear, restores the spirit, calms the breast, feeds the soul, and gives rest, it *tends the child*—looking forward to the end of stanza 4. This is our primal experience of the mother love that makes everything all right, so the name of Jesus.

Some of this sense of the child, needing comfort, healing, soothing, is lost in the common alteration of *his* to *our.* In the Lutheran and Episcopal inclusive version, the connection between "a believer's ear" (singular) and "our" sorrows, wounds, and fears (plural) is confused. The mother whispers the comforting name into the individual ear, one at a time. (The Catholic version substitutes an audience.) The collective *our* generalizes, abstracting the experience. The Lutheran substitution of *heart's unrest* and the Catholic *troubled mind* for *troubled breast* are similarly annoying. The modern editorial challenge is that of combining poetic integrity with politic inclusiveness. Unless the metaphor is clear, inclusive edits will fail the text. A child's "troubled breast" sobs and heaves visibly; the "heart's unrest" seems to call for a stethoscope and a sedative; a "troubled mind" needs therapy.

At the same time that the first two stanzas, as originally written, invoke our universal childhood experience, they also make subtle reference to that network of biblical experience that enlarges and extends hymn poetry. The "name like perfume" and the "love of the maidens" are just below the surface. Wounded spirits, troubled breasts, and rest for the weary are all familiar to lovers as well as infants. The "manna" for the hungry soul most carefully reminds us that the beloved children, comforted, are also the children of God, wandering dependents in the wilderness.

The third stanza becomes more assertive. *I* replaces *the name* as the grammatical subject. The name as the rock on which "I build" suggests adult activity and judgment, although the need for a "shield and hiding-place" marks a partial retreat from confidence. The language is particularly reminiscent of psalm metaphors for security. The name as treasury, filled with "stores," is basically a new item (although related to the "portion"), suggesting wealth and riches of the name of Jesus. The range of metaphor, like the power of the name, is startling.*

The fourth stanza of seven is, appropriately, central. Here we articulate the role of Jesus as mediator, learning by explaining, following standard hymn pedagogy. We have moved from a survey of common experience of the broad power of Jesus' name to the concise explanation of how this all happens: "By thee my prayers acceptance gain, / Although with sin defiled." This mediation, despite sin, is the power source for all the many metaphorical activities of the name. It is *why* the name is sweet in the believer's ear, *how* it works to comfort and heal and feed and relieve. The mediation of Jesus with his Father works despite the fouling by sin of our petitions—*defiled* is a strong, repellent word—and despite terrible Satanic accusation—again, a strong, frightening idea. Finally, and most importantly, the mediation is what culminates in God's acknowledgment of me as child—recalling and reinforcing the images of infancy comforted in the first two stanzas. When the Episcopalians and Catholics cut stanza 4, they edited out Christ the mediator.

We are not, of course, the children of Jesus, but a suitable metaphor for our relationship to him is desirable in this hymn which is a lesson in words, their effect and significance. In the fifth stanza, Newton summons a series of traditional metaphors, each packed with significance, so familiar from Bible stories, iconography, and everyday experience that it would be tedious to detail them. The "Husband" metaphor—which *all* the hymnals have replaced with *Guardian*—belongs here for several reasons: it refers to the source text of the hymn and consolidates the love language of sweetness and dearness and security; it is an important item in the Christian tradition which has been deeply meaningful to millions of believers, including our best women poets; and it is one item only in a list of ten metaphors, so that singers for whom it means nothing have other options. (One might

---

* The Catholic substitutions of plural pronouns are unnecessary, perhaps the fault of a mistaken idea of "subjectivity." So, too, the preference for *Blest name!* rather than *Dear name* seems to want to avoid sentiment. But the substitution of *resting place* for *hiding place* is oddly passive and the replacement of *treasury* with *comfort* is weak. (A "comfort" filled with "blessings of his Grace" is metaphorically impenetrable.)

also argue that to appreciate the metaphor one needn't have a loving, supportive husband any more than one need be a sheep to praise the shepherd or live under a wise monarch to praise the King.) *Guardian* of the altered version is vague, neither familiar nor visible to the mind's eye. If *husband* is still objectionable, I would suggest, given the nurturant imagery, that an alteration more in keeping with the text as it was written would be "O Jesus, shepherd, mother, friend."[*]

The prayers which gain acceptance through the mediation of Jesus (stanza 4) and the praise I bring (stanza 5) are verbal formulations. Prayers and praise use words, as does this hymn I am singing, however defiled (in the case of the prayers) or provisional and chaotic (in the case of the ten metaphors). The "name of Jesus," as sweet sounding and efficacious, is implicitly contrasted to our own attempts at expression, which were signaled by the introduction of the first-person subject in the third stanza (except in the GIA version, which missed the point). This tacit critique of our own words, in contrast to the power of the name of Jesus, becomes explicit in stanza 6—cut, with the balance of Newton's text, by the Catholics. This critique is as conventional as the ten metaphors, and we recall the frustration of the psalmist and countless devotional poets who have regretted their inability to express the inexpressible. Because hymns are collective expressions, Newton's confession of inability is at once the poet's and every singer's. That "the effort of my heart" to praise is "weak" and that "my warmest thought" is "cold" takes us back to our distressed childhood as believers and singers in the first stanzas. The final revelation will enable our proper praise. (This stanza is the very inappropriate conclusion to the Episcopal text.)

The final stanza bravely refuses to be dejected by the weakness and coldness of mortal praise. It accepts the mortal terms of praise in quite extraordinary fashion. "I *would* thy love proclaim" expresses the *will*, however human, to unceasing proclamation and praise. That we do this

---

[*] That Lutheran editors failed to appreciate the metaphors as unique and vital analogies, familiar from tradition, is further evident in their failure to capitalize *life, way,* and *end.* These are, no less than the others, sturdy, giant ideas. The separation of *Lord* from this series discourages our contemplation of *Lord* as a word or referent to something that cannot be isolated and exactly named—which is one ingenious feature of the original text.

"with every fleeting breath" emphasizes the physiology of speech and song (exhalation) at the same time that it insists on the transience of life—the breaths with which we sing mortal songs are numbered and fleeting. Both music and death are contained in the image of "fleeting breath."

Our need for refreshment in death brings deathbed scenes to mind, the comfort of quite specific food and drink and medicine. The name which soothed sorrows, healed wounds, dispelled fear, is still protective, recalling the nurture of the first two stanzas. The subtle narrative thread of a life, from infancy to death, ends, like a movie, with music. Just possibly the mothering name conveys some sense of Mary the mother, petitioned to be "with us now and in the hour of our death," when weakness and coldness are no longer merely metaphors for mortality.

Glorious Things of Thee Are Spoken

In "Zion, or the City of God" (or "Glorious Things of Thee Are Spoken")—sung by all but the Catholics—Newton displays the City of God before his singers, using the tableau techniques we have noted in other hymns. This hymn is at once the descendant of biblical prophecy and a poetic ancestor of the Hollywood biblical spectacular:

Zion, or the City of God

1. GLORIOUS things of thee are spoken,
   Zion, city of our God!
   He, whose word cannot be broken,
   Form'd thee for his own abode;
   On the Rock of ages founded,
   What can shake thy sure repose?
   With salvation's walls surrounded,
   Thou may'st smile at all thy foes.

2. See! the streams of living waters,
   Springing from eternal love,
   Well supply thy sons and daughters,
   And all fear of want remove;

Who can faint while such a river
Ever flows their thrist [*sic*] t' assuage?
Grace which, like the Lord the giver,
Never fails from age to age.

3. Round each habitation hov'ring,
See the cloud and fire appear!
For a glory and a cov'ring,
Shewing that the Lord is near;
Thus deriving from their banner,
Light by night, and shade by day;
Safe they feed upon the manna
Which he gives them when they pray.

4. Bless'd inhabitants of Zion,
Wash'd in the Redeemer's blood!
Jesus, whom their souls rely on,
Makes them kings and priests to God.
'Tis his love his people raises
Over self to reign as kings,
And as priests, his solemn praises
Each for a thank-off'ring brings.

5. Saviour if of Zion's city
I thro' grace a member am;
Let the world deride or pity,
I will glory in thy name;
Fading is the worldling's pleasure,
All his boasted pomp and show;
Solid joys and lasting treasure,
None but Zion's children know.

We first observe how the longer, fuller stanzas give a broader scope to the hymn as poem, a breadth reinforced by the familiar Haydn tune. While four-line stanzas of several hymn texts we have studied before this were combined to yield eight-line forms, this is the first hymn we have treated in which the thought is continued through the eight-line unit. Newton needed the longer stanzas to work through the challenge of this hymn to dramatize and interpret rich and complicated biblical experience.

The hymn opens with a report, addressed to Zion, of its fame. This is a reasonable starting point: However confused we may be about Zion, we have certainly all heard glorious things about it. (The original "Glorious things" is a less archaic and artificial expression than the new Lutheran "Glories of your name." Furthermore, the name, substituted for the city itself as the object of praise, diffuses the idea.) The address to Zion effectively conveys the personification of the city—an ancient tradition, familiar from Scripture. Accordingly, in the following lines images of the city as an architectural monument combine impressively with such personification. The abode, the foundation upon the Rock, the walls are all architectural, while the sure repose, the smiling, and the idea of having foes are human, qualities of some person we might address.

Beyond the city's fame and its human face, the hymn reports on the city's formation and security. Major league metaphors are incorporated—the city as the abode of God, the Rock of ages as foundation and the walls of salvation. However, Newton is very careful to keep the sense of the hymn from depending upon these allusions, which are actually relatively difficult ideas. A second set of messages, reinforcing the main story line, provides lessons in faith and hope: the word of God cannot be broken; the peace of the city is sure; foes may be contemned.

The initial "See!" of stanza 2 signals the beginning of an impressive spectacle. We again note how Newton carefully balances the esoteric symbolic figure of "streams of living waters, / Springing from eternal love" with common, familiar experience. The living waters and love eternal are unexceptionable, powerful images. They need the tangible immediacy of the backup pictures, however, the simple "sons and daughters" who "fear want" and know ordinary water well. By means of this juxtaposition, the living waters are at once a high symbol of eternal life and the metropolitan water works of Zion city. The streams—as spring as drink—become, in the end, the river of unfailing grace. Grand symbol and ordinary water flow together in the poetry.

In the next stanza we move from water to the sky of Exodus, with its pillar of cloud and fire. Now all four classical elements have been invoked to describe Zion—water, earth, air, and fire. Our experience of water that lets us understand the river of grace in stanza 2 now cedes to the experience of Zion in the wilderness, presumably even there the "City of God." The injunction of the second line to "See" indicates the continuation of the spectacle. As the sons and daughters were given water to drink in the previous stanza, now they are fed from heaven.

The first three stanzas have kept us at a spectator's distance from Zion, a distance that closes a bit as the hymn proceeds. The first stanza had us reporting rumored things and wondering—as outsiders—at the peace and security of the city. In the second we envied the city's sons and daughters in general on the city services. In the third we admired the more specific care and protection accorded the people of God in the wilderness. The cumulative effect is to make us *want* to belong to this people. This is the designed response which comes most clear in the important fourth stanza.[*] Now the inhabitants of Zion are clearly the Christian community, "Wash'd in the Redeemer's Blood." The water has become blood. In his love, Jesus has reordered the government, making the inhabitants "kings and priests." This, finally—here in the fourth stanza—seems to be *our* community, audibly identifiable as ours because, with this hymn, *we* sing praises as thank-offerings. Here, after three stanzas of distance, we join in the activity of the city of Zion. (Almost needless to say, when the Lutherans cut this stanza, they excised the climax of the hymn.)

The final stanza formulates our response to the preceding vision. Reflecting his Calvinist concern about election, Newton wrote, "Saviour *if* of Zion's city / I thro' grace a member am." For non-Calvinist singers (in fact, only the Lutherans are still singing), *if* is properly altered to *since*. This original worry, however, enhances our appreciation of the longing to belong that seemed to intensify through the course of the first four stanzas. Whatever my attitude toward election, the hymn has me declare how citi-

---

[*] Methodist editors failed to appreciate this movement, the restraint which heightens our desire, and rush the identification, substituting *our* and *we* and *us* for *their* and *they* and *them*. The Presbyterians end with stanza 3, stopping short of the all-important identification of us, the singers, with Zion.

zenship, through grace, removes me from worldly attitudes and judgments. My attitude toward the pleasures of this world and its display is altered.

This introduction of a counterview, a rejection of the world, entails a tricky change in direction. The world of Zion has dominated the hymn, luring us into belonging. Only here at the end does the secular world intrude with its challenge, deriding and pitying. The rumors of glorious things, the absoluteness of the city, the tableaux from the past and the liveliness of the city of the redeemed—these had all seemed so absolute and beyond question. In fact it is our experience of the city, through the hymn, that has taught us to look down on the lesser pleasures and display of this world. The last stanza gives us the desired yield, our final, proper benefits of citizenship in Zion.

God Moves in a Mysterious Way

William Cowper is the first of the hymn writers whose work we treat in these pages who has been generally recognized by literary historians as a serious poet. (Quite evidently, I feel that literary historians have erred in their neglect of Watts, but that's really beside the point here.) Cowper also stands apart from his hymn-writing colleagues and predecessors as a layman and as a man who was deeply disturbed, mentally and spiritually. (These two distinguishing characteristics are not always linked.) Cowper's hymns are lovely and difficult, tending toward a personal vision rather than that exemplary, constructive, responsive script for believers which is the hymn norm. It is sad, but no wonder that Cowper's work is out of favor. "God Moves in a Mysterious Way" is only sung by Lutherans, Episcopalians, and Presbyterians.

Light Shining Out of Darkness

1. GOD moves in a mysterious way,
     His wonders to perform;
     He plants his footsteps in the sea,
     And rides upon the storm.

2. Deep in unfathomable mines
   Of never failing skill,
   He treasures up his bright designs,
   And works his sov'reign will.

3. Ye fearful saints, fresh courage take;
   The clouds ye so much dread
   Are big with mercy, and shall break
   In blessings on your head.

4. Judge not the LORD by feeble sense,
   But trust him for his grace;
   Beneath a frowning providence
   He hides a smiling face.

5. His purposes will ripen fast,
   Unfolding every hour;
   The bud may have a bitter taste,
   But sweet will be the flower.

6. Blind unbelief is sure to err,
   And scan his works in vain:
   GOD is his own interpreter,
   And he will make it plain.

If this hymn is really a celebration of "light shining out of darkness," it's not a visible light! The title seems an item of wishful thinking, as is the hymn text, a hoping against hope that the darkness and misery of life aren't real, that the apparent frightfulness of God is a misapprehension. This is gripping but not particularly edifying or even helpful.

The first stanza, largely untouched by editors, gives us two extraordinary pictures of God. God's "moving" recalls the spirit moving on the waters. Yet, when he moves in a way that is mysterious, the words mean several things at once—the way or path is a puzzle, impossible to follow; his movement is puzzling or, alternatively, characteristic of a solemn rite or "mystery." Actually, it's the gestures of a magician that are most notably "mysterious," and it is such a magician that the second line confirms, a god, who "performs wonders," amazing tricks. Since these aren't described or itemized, we're left with a vague idea. The magician cedes in the following two lines to a picture of the classical god Poseidon or Neptune or, possibly, a Nordic or Germanic counterpart. These are the familiar giant figures who cross the sea and ride the storm. They are frightening and malicious, threatening devastation.

The two pictures, of magician and sea god, converge by means of their shared imagery. The spirit that moved (mysteriously) on the waters in the first line anticipates the Neptune figure, with his giant footsteps, in the third. The way-as-path anticipates the footsteps and the rider. The sum is a gripping and disturbing montage of our fears and fascinations. The only hopeful item is the verb *plants,* which generally suggests life and growing things and promise. Here, however, God "plants his footsteps in the sea," not a very hopeful seedbed. (The Presbyterian version has the singers address this odd deity, telling him what he does rather than reporting on his activities. The alteration, doubtless intended to get around the male pronouns, intensifies the strangeness.)

In the second stanza, deleted by Lutherans, we plunge from the height of the storm to the depths of the mines. The bowels of the earth and the bright and intricate treasures of the ancient barrow or hoard traditionally belong to Hephaistos or Vulcan, another classical deity. Hephaistos's skill was unfailing and he produced a trove of "bright designs." He crafted armor for heroes, beautiful drinking cups, and the famous net in which he trapped his wife, Aphrodite, with her lover, Ares. The application of such an idea to the Christian God is interesting but unorthodox. The "treasuring up" is hoarding, also the ungenerous activity of gnomes. "Designs" are plans, not complete and fulfilled works, not glories or manifest goodness. The "sovereign will" God "works" is, like the mines, unfathomable. (Again, the Presbyterian address *to* such a god seems more radical than Cowper's original description of God using these classical models.)

These mines are "unfathomable" in several senses—immeasurably deep, unintelligible, impenetrable, unembraceable. We just can't understand or relate. *Unfathomable,* like *never failing* is a negative formulation.

These are collecting at an alarming rate. The heights were dark, thanks to the storm, unillumined by sun or moon or stars. The depths are only questionably lit by "bright designs." Where is this "light shining out of darkness" anyway?

The Lutheran elimination of stanza 2 is understandable, but it ruins the progression of ideas. Indeed, stanza 3 turns to comfort the saints, who have every right to be fearful. The dreaded clouds, on which God rode in stanza 1, *will* break in blessings. Cowper has us *insist* on this, providing no reason, no evidence, no picture to balance the terrifying pagan images he has conjured. All we have to go on is the suspicion of our senses and the need to trust God, the ideas of stanza 4. It would seem that "fresh courage" needs a livelier source. The blessings of rainfall to plant life might have worked, for example. But here Cowper can only suggest a sort of bad joker god who pretends he's going to blast us but instead breaks blessings on our head—not really a very pleasant image at all.

Stanza 4 at first view seems to insist that we not judge the Lord, a venerable and righteous idea. But actually, that's not exactly what Cowper is saying. He says we aren't to judge the Lord "by feeble sense." In other words, we mustn't trust what we see or hear or taste or smell or feel. The evidence of our senses, which are limited and weak, will convince us, wrongly, that God means us no good. In fact, the imagery of the poem itself suggests God's pagan cruelty. Through its images, poetry appeals to our "feeble sense." The evidence—of experience and literature—by which we might be tempted to judge God is all *against* his grace. We can only trust.

God as a sort of terrible cosmic trickster comes clear in the last two lines of stanza 4. Providence is regularly personified in eighteenth-century religious poetry, so the "frowning Providence" is presumably a mask, angry and disapproving. What we *see* and know of God is not at all nice or ingratiating. The God of history is dreadful. But, doubting our senses and all our experience, we ought to trust that, beneath the mask is a nice God. The "smiling face" is profoundly and, I think, unintentionally, ambiguous. God smiles graciously indeed, but if his kindness is invisible, we are still at a loss. If, moreover, I am convinced he is conning me, terrifying me unnecessarily with his cruel mask, then his smile is the sinister smile of the bully who's scared a victim. (The edits in the Lutheran version don't begin to deal with the crisis in the poetry; the Presbyterian deletion of stanza 4 is reasonable.)

The fifth stanza, cut by the Lutherans and the Presbyterians, gives us the first natural, gracious imagery of the hymn. Here we have God's purpose as a fruit, ripening. Bitter buds will become sweet flowers. The analogies are sensuous—sight, taste, smell—hence suspicious. (We should remember that our senses are feeble and no grounds for judgment.) Their usefulness as reassurance that all is under control is further undermined by the unnatural speed of the ripening—*unfolding every hour* suggests late-breaking news, crises in progress, rather than the measured progress of natural growth. So the "bitter taste" of the bud is a given while the sweet flower is only something to look forward to. In fact the whole organic process is out of order, with the ripening first, then unfolding, then buds, then flowers. As an illustration of the trust mandated in the preceding stanza, stanza 5 is unreliable.

The final stanza, which we all sing, confirms the desperate confusion. Now "unbelief" is personified as "blind" and "sure to err." Have we forgotten that Belief (or Trust) was supposed to be blind, willfully ignoring the evil evidence all around, trusting that "frowning Providence" was just a mask? Here, *unbelief* attempts to draw conclusions about God from the study of nature, seen as a scholarly or scientific task, investigating the works of God. This attempt is vain for unbelief—*as it was vain for belief.* No human being, believing Christian or unbeliever, Cowper seems to say, can make any sense of the darkness.

The last two lines sound good, but what are they saying? Quite literally, only God knows. That God does interpret what we scan in vain is a matter of trust. We don't even know what *it* means, as in "he will make it plain." The pronoun *it* has no antecedent. Since Cowper was too good a poet for this to be an accident, a grammatical lapse, perhaps we should read it as a bitter joke. The absence of evident meaning in God's activity ultimately undermines even the language of our poetry about faith.

VI: Nineteenth-Century Hymnody: Literary and Liturgical

urning to English hymnody of the nineteenth century, we gain admission to Anglican worship. For more than a century, hymns had, in the Church of England, been associated with dissent and Methodism, with the mob of religious enthusiasts and evangelicals. The hymns of Bishop Reginald Heber (1783–1826) and John Mason Neale (1818–1866) made hymnody acceptable in the Church of England. We accordingly sample these texts.

Brightest and Best of the Stars of the Morning

"Brightest and Best" is very pretty. Such prettiness is endorsed as an elegant relief by those who see in Bishop Heber, at last, a champion of poetical hymnody. Lutherans, Episcopalians, and Presbyterians all sing versions close to the original, found in Heber's *Hymns, Written and Adapted to the Weekly Church Service of the Year* (1827).

Epiphany.—No II.

1. Brightest and best of the sons of the morning!
      Dawn on our darkness and lend us thine aid!
   Star of the East, the horizon adorning,
      Guide where our infant Redeemer is laid!

2. Cold on his cradle the dewdrops are shining,
      Low lies his head with the beasts of the stall,
   Angels adore him in slumber reclining,
      Maker and Monarch and Saviour of all!

3. Say, shall we yield him, in costly devotion,
      Odours of Edom and offerings divine?
   Gems of the mountain and pearls of the ocean,
      Myrrh from the forest or gold from the mine?

4. Vainly we offer each ample oblation;
      Vainly with gifts would his favour secure:
   Richer by far is the heart's adoration;
      Dearer to God are the prayers of the poor.

5. Brightest and best of the sons of the morning!
      Dawn on our darkness and lend us thine aid!
   Star of the East, the horizon adorning,
      Guide where our infant Redeemer is laid!

All of us begin the first line by addressing the *star* which will guide us to Bethlehem. But who were those original *sons*—as stars—of the morning? We have to stop and think for a moment. The sun is certainly a star that rises in the east in the morning, the brightest and best of the morning stars. The sun suggests, always, the Son, but that's problematic here, since Jesus is more than simply the brightest and best of a number of sons. That seems to be a false trail. There's powerful mythology behind this start, nevertheless, however incomplete the commitment to it. The morning star is Venus, love personified, and a powerful tradition backs up the morning star (or *Morgenstern*) as a type of Christ, influencing our lives with all the power the stars were believed to exert. The morning herself is Aurora, the female deity of the dawn.

Certainly the alteration of *sons* to "*stars* of the morning" is a distraction, forcing us to address the brightest of the stars as such, without any larger frame of association, without the suggestion that this star is Christ the son. In the first half of the first stanza, we the singers identify with the Magi, who, obviously, believed in the significance of the stars and were prone to recognize such heavenly signs. (Although the Magi might have addressed a star, this seems like a questionable address in a Christian hymn.) The second line sustains the double association of star with Jesus, as both himself and as a sign. The star, *as star,* doesn't "dawn on our darkness and lend us [its] aid" certainly. The infant's birth is such a dawning. So, lost in the stars, we miss the son.

In the second half of the stanza, while we continue to impersonate the Magi, we are more clearly a Christian people who know that this is our "infant Redeemer." The star, no longer "dawning on our darkness" or "lending us thine aid," is separated from the child, an *adornment* merely.

The prettiness of this text, despite its confusion, is partly a function of its Latinate diction, of how and when Heber uses elegant words like *adorn, infant, adore, recline,* and, of course, *oblation.* This begins to come clear already in the second half of the first stanza. *Horizon adorning* is elegantly decorative rather than forceful or visible or even significant. So *infant Redeemer* is elegant in contrast to *Christchild* or *Baby Jesus.* (*Infant* and *Redeemer* are both Latinate and relatively arcane words.) That the infant "is laid," a passive construction, without any clue as to the agent, is likewise a bit effete. (Nobody's *doing* anything.) The first half of the stanza, in contrast, employed a more Germanic (Anglo-Saxon) vocabulary of familiar monosyllables.

I must confess that the dewdrops shining cold on the cradle have bothered me since my own infancy. A manger may serve as a cradle, but it remains a manger. And well might we ask why there are dewdrops on the cradle if it's inside the stable. Further, we might wonder why they're "shining." I think that the only answer is the effort at prettiness: the dewdrops are meant as decoration (hence their shining) and a "cradle" is sweeter than a manger. Its finished wood is also more apt to display those dewdrops to advantage.

Unfortunately, the troubles don't stop with the dewdrops or a child's questions: the line "Low lies his head with the beasts of the stall" also challenges the adult singer. The idea, clearly, is that Jesus humbled himself, but the picture is problematic. It almost suggests that his head is lower than his body, and, since "beasts" are large and take up considerable vertical space, the positioning is unclear. (If the baby, not just his head, were lying low, this would not be quite so confusing.) The Latinate depiction of the baby "in slumber reclining" makes matters worse. Of course babies simply *don't* "recline" in "slumber." (They just lie there sleeping, with luck.) *Reclining* suggests lying back at an angle, in this case, unfortunately, head down. Finally, it seems to me that the adoration of the angels and the summary greatness of "Maker and Monarch and Saviour of all" only reminds us that an epiphany hymn should properly explain these three roles ("Maker" in particular) and ignore the stars and dewdrops.

In the third stanza, Heber has us, with the Magi, ponder appropriate offering to the Child. The language is artificial: to "yield" gifts is very strange and "costly devotion" is difficult, depending on the obscure meaning of *devotion* as "gift" as well as the more normal "worship." "Odours of Edom" belong completely to the Magi as they would never occur to most of us as a likely gift. "Offerings divine" is nonspecific. (In fact, *offerings* would even seem, by definition, non-divine.) The sources of the gems and pearls and myrrh and gold in mountain, ocean, forest, and mine, respectively, don't seem particularly useful bits of information either. The stanza enjoys itself, nevertheless, sharing with singers a pleasure in reviewing exotic possibilities. This is, it seems to me, prettiness at the expense of poetic economy. In other words, singers who, through repetition, commit these lines to memory gain little of lasting devotional or educational value.

The Latinate judgment on such gifts that introduces the following stanza is almost impenetrable: "Vainly we offer each ample oblation" is next to meaningless. Pearls and odors aren't "ample" in any usual sense, and an "oblation" is simply puzzling. Despite the parallel structure ("Vainly . . ."), the next line introduces an entirely different idea without explaining what's meant. Have we been trying to "secure his favour" with our gifts? So far they seemed to have been forthright offerings. (We note the Latinisms in passing.) Our vanity seems to have two good, clear senses, however—what we do is *both* "vain" in the sense of "to no purpose" *and* an expression of our vanity as pride.

The obscure Latin words of the first two lines of stanza 4 are balanced by the homeliness of the second two, which one might read as an ironic verbal sign that in his heart Heber knew how God wants us to speak clearly and forthrightly! Our artificiality—as Magi or poets—like our "oblation," is vain. *Rich* and *dear* are nicely juxtaposed here. The "heart's adoration" is richer than fancy gifts; the "prayers of the poor" are dearer than ample oblations. *Dear,* of course, means both costly and beloved.

As the Presbyterians evidently recognize, the return to the beginning stanza in the end is unsatisfactory, canceling any progress we might have made from Latinate glitz to the value of forthright prayer. In fact, the identification of the star with the infant is still incomplete, and our identification with the Magi and their costly gifts has been challenged, judged vain and inconsequential compared to the prayers of the poor. Why, we might ask, do we keep up the pretense?

Holy, Holy, Holy

Heber's "Brightest and Best" seemed to assume that its singers had a pretty good grasp of stars and Magi, of incarnational theology and Latinate vocabulary. Elegance and prettiness, in poetry as in life, demand a certain leisure, a relief from the pressure of evangelical communication and devotional instruction. I think we can observe the same set of assumptions in his "Holy, Holy, Holy!" Singers seem to have to know a lot. Here, however, the hymn is complicated by the incantatory repetition, with the saints, of the Sanctus woven into the text. As with "Brightest and Best," the very long verse lines add to the leisurely, measured feel. (All our sample hymnals include this hymn.)

Trinity Sunday

1. Holy, holy, holy, Lord God Almighty!
    Early in the morning our song shall rise to Thee;
  Holy, holy, holy! merciful and mighty!
    God in three persons, blessed Trinity!

2. Holy, holy, holy! all the saints adore Thee,
    Casting down their golden crowns around the glassy sea;
  Cherubim and seraphim falling down before Thee,
    Which wert and art and evermore shalt be!

3. Holy, holy, holy! Though the darkness hide Thee,
    Though the eye of sinful man Thy glory may not see,
  Only Thou art holy, there is none beside Thee,
    Perfect in power, in love, and purity!

4. Holy, holy, holy, Lord God Almighty!
    All Thy works shall praise Thy name in earth and sky
      and sea.
  Holy, holy, holy! merciful and mighty!
    God in three persons, blessed Trinity!

While the hymn is intended for "Trinity Sunday," it is immediately apparent that Heber doesn't feel that his singers need any special help with the doctrine of the Trinity. The hymn is rather more a worship formula than instruction in devotional response familiar from the hymns of Watts and Wesley and Newton. This suggests a new understanding of what hymns are and how they work. As they were a part of a liturgy, their autonomy as texts, their self-sufficiency, was less compelling. I think that this hymn also marks a fresh attempt to *express* praise. Rather than explaining why we should, telling us how we should, or provoking us to praise, Heber looks for words that seem to capture and articulate the act itself. We have already suggested that this is difficult, if not impossible.

The first stanza directs us through a formulaic adoration of the Holy Trinity. *Holy,* the word, repeated over and over again in this stanza and throughout the hymn, becomes a kind of incantation whereby singers acknowledge that God is holy. The incantation is, presumably, modeled on the behavior of the angels in Revelation and the creatures in Isaiah. It doesn't really *mean* anything and doesn't seem to have to: of course God is holy, by definition. If we didn't understand the idea, we wouldn't be in church singing the hymn. The end.

What would we think, though, of a *congregational* hymn that consisted of nothing but *Holy!* repeated over and over, beginning to end, or *Alleluia!* not as a refrain, not as our lines in a larger drama, but as the whole thing? I don't think that would work. We want more. Hymn texts still must shape and define our worship, even if we all know the basics of the faith and want a more straightforward expression of praise and adoration. The genre of the hymn makes such demands, raises such expectations.

Indeed such shaping happens in this hymn. There's more here than just everlasting "holies." The first stanza, with its affirmation, reminds us of and reinforces familiar ideas. We begin with the acclamation of the triple holiness of the "Lord God Almighty," a name so familiar it's a commonplace oath. (It's even possible that some of the exclamation of the oath plays into the hymn. We begin with the holiness of what we often hear profaned.) While the second line is the only line of the stanza that contains a declarative sentence, it's ambiguous: Is *shall* used in the sense of "should" (our song *should* or *ought to* rise)? Or does it indicate futurity (that's what we'll do)? Is it a report or an injunction or a promise? And what morning are we talking about? Every morning or Sunday morning or Easter morning or the morning of the new day of revelation? It's not clear. If we presume that the song that is to rise is this one we're singing, then this is a report on what we're doing now. That's a bit odd, if we stop to think about it.

In the third line, mercy and (somewhat redundantly) might are apparently ascribed to "Thee," the Lord God Al*mighty*. But the grammar isn't really very clear here either. Perhaps God is being addressed *as* these adjectives, cut off from the foregoing. The length of the lines and their independence, as exclamations, one from another tend to divide the thought up into single-line units. Certainly neither the might nor the mercy of God are further developed or itemized or related to one another or to holiness.

It seems that this grammatical fragmentation and avoidance of declarative sentences is a part of the exclamatory, affirmative nature of this hymn. The last line shows how it's worked: the "three persons" connect with the repeated triple repetition of *Holy,* one *Holy* for each person. It seems that this association is supposed to happen in the singer's mind, imprinted through repetition. Since it isn't explained, we must conclude that such explanation must not have seemed called for. Heber's singers either must have made the association by themselves or not have cared especially what was going on.

In the second stanza, according to this reading, "Holy, holy, holy," presumably now standing for—interchangeable with—the "blessed Trinity" of the preceding line, *is* the "Thee" whom all the saints adore. The acclamation "Holy, holy, holy" *has become* "God in three persons." But perhaps we've taken the triple *Holy* too seriously as an expression of the Trinity. If that's so, then the triple *Holy* in the first line of the second stanza is *what* "all the saints" sing when they "adore Thee." The grammar of the line lets us go either way, which is confusing.

The confusion is especially bothersome in a stanza which seems intended to provide a vision, an apocalyptic spectacle of saints and crowns and glassy sea. Spectacles, we have learned, need to be very clearly drawn to do their work. Here the central attraction is unclear. Is it the glassy sea surrounded by those crowns or the ineffable "Thee" before whom the angels fall? The cherubim and seraphim (assuming we know what they are) are doubtless very lovely in their worship, but Heber doesn't help us see them.

The last line makes it clear that the "Thee" whom they worship is eternal, the God of past, present, and future. Typically, this familiar formula demands considerable theological understanding, and one can't be sure that this idea of eternity—which is not explained or even mentioned elsewhere in the text—would come clear to most singers. Indeed the whole picture is strange, if biblical, and assumes familiarity. It recalls the ambiguity of the second line of the first stanza, where we couldn't tell exactly what *shall* meant. Perhaps Heber's effort at representing *eternal* praise was just more than language could bear. Poets, even the psalmist, have suggested it's not possible. The Catholic substitution of "God everlasting through eternity" seems moderately redundant (*everlasting* means "through eternity") and leaves out the past and present ("wert and art") instead of updating them.

The third stanza retreats from the vision (which was never too clear anyway) of the second stanza. After all the spectacle and the singing with the saints, we're back in the dark, God is hidden, and we, as sinful, cannot see God's glory. The early morning of the first stanza, when we shall raise our song, is gone too. We may well wonder what happened! As if that weren't disappointing enough, the grammar gets all tangled up as well. The *though*s, meaning "although," are unrelated to the following clauses. How is God's hiddenness and our sinful blindness related to the affirmations that "Thou art holy" and "there is none beside Thee"? We can only speculate that we *affirm* and *believe* these things despite our lack of empirical evidence. This sounds much like poor Cowper's distress at the unpleasant appearance of things.

Certainly the affirmations, the latest in the long series, that "only Thou art holy" and "there is none beside thee" and that thou art "perfect in power, in love, and purity" are not meant for reflection or explication. They won't be explained or illustrated or brought home. They are simply theological declarations, familiar or unfamiliar, juxtaposed with the triple *Holy* and rehearsed as worship. God as "perfect in power," for example, sounds right, but doesn't take us much beyond the *Almighty* of the first line of the first stanza. (*Perfect in Power* is simply a pompous Latinate version of *Almighty*.) *Love* and *purity* haven't been considered.

The only new item in the last stanza is the psalm verse "All Thy works shall praise Thy name. . . ." Presumably that's what we've been doing, praising the *name,* and that's what we ought to do. While Newton, treating the name of Jesus, worked us through the metaphorical tangle, Heber short-circuits the discussion and tries to just have us do it. Syntax is irrelevant and ambiguity untroubling. This recalls Charles Wesley's confusion of metaphor, the rush of ideas that somehow expressed the collapse of logic characteristic of religious experience. Either Heber was more of an evangelical enthusiast than is generally thought or less of a poet. Shall we, along with the other works of God, really praise the name of the Trinity "in earth and sky and sea"? The suggestion is bizarre in its call for a busy schedule of swimming and flying and digging by all God's works. Heber must have meant that all God's works, "in earth and sky and sea"—animals, birds, fish, all creatures—shall praise "Thy name." A good poet gets the grammar right.

Oh, Come, Oh, Come, Emmanuel

John Mason Neale's original Advent hymn, "Oh, Come, Oh, Come, Emmanuel," first published in 1851 in his *Medieval Hymns and Sequences,* was a translation of selected Latin antiphons. It is framed as a series of metaphors, carefully linked together. While all our hymnals contain some version of "Oh, Come," each is a different mixture of antiphons, variously ascribed to different translators. The stanzas have been heavily altered and rearranged and supplemented. The most obvious shared alteration is the change from "Draw nigh, draw nigh" to "Oh, come, oh, come," a change evidently called for by a musical setting that insisted upon an unaccented syllable followed by an accented.

Veni, Veni, Emmanuel

1. Draw nigh, draw nigh, Emmanuel,
   And loose Thy captive Israel,
   That mourns in lonely exile here,
   Until the SON of GOD appear!
       Rejoice! rejoice! Emmanuel
       Is born for thee, O Israel!

2.   O Rod of Jesse's stem, arise,
     And free us from our enemies,
     And set us loose from Satan's chains,
     And from the pit with all its pains!
          Rejoice! rejoice! Emmanuel
          Is born for thee, O Israel!

3.   Thou, the true East, draw nigh, draw nigh,
     To give us comfort from on high!
     And drive away the shades of night,
     And pierce the clouds, and bring us light!
          Rejoice! rejoice! Emmanuel
          Is born for thee, O Israel!

4.   Key of the House of David, come!
     Reopen Thou our heavenly home!
     Make safe the way that we must go,
     And close the path that leads below.
          Rejoice! rejoice! Emmanuel
          Is born for thee, O Israel!

5.   Ruler and LORD, draw nigh, draw nigh!
     Who to thy flock in Sinai
     Didst give, of ancient times, Thy Law,
     In cloud and majesty and awe.
          Rejoice! rejoice! Emmanuel
          Is born for thee, O Israel!

The considerable subtlety of this hymn is first and most clearly instanced in the balance between each stanza and the refrain. The body of each stanza petitions the action of the Lord in a series of metaphors and metaphorical functions: Emmanuel, do this; Rod of Jesse, do this; true East, do this; Key of the House of David, do this; Ruler and Lord, do this. The stanzas are urgent requests for present action. The refrain, in contrast, answers the requests with assurance and reassurance of the completion of the promise in the birth that has already happened. Our anxious, urgent pleading is soothed. This emotional dynamic, the interplay between urgent need and confidence, accurately reflects the tension of Advent when we summon up all the anticipation of the Messiah, all the while knowing that Emmanuel *is born*.

In practical terms, this pattern of shifting address means that the stanzas have us, as Israel, address the Lord in various traditional metaphorical capacities while the refrain turns us to urge Israel to rejoice in the good news. In their refrain, the revised versions obscure this dynamic as they put the birth—not even exactly a birth but another vague "come"—in the future. Instead of us as singers proclaiming to Israel that "Emmanuel *is* born for thee," we sing that "Emmanuel *shall come to* thee." This futurity replaces the confident assurance of the original and unbalances the hymn.

In the first stanza, *Draw nigh,* for all its archaism, is a petition for the close-coming of Emmanuel, "God with us." As such, it insists upon our intimacy with the Savior, who must not only "come" but come near enough to do all that we require. These activities, for which the Lord must come close, are the substance of the lines and stanzas that follow. The "loosing" of Israel is to be the leading metaphor. Israel is modified by *thy*—appropriately, the Lord's people—and by its captivity, hence "Thy captive Israel." The idea of *ransom,* introduced in all the modern texts ("And ransom captive Israel") simply doesn't fit here: it's a different metaphor, having to do with cost and purchase rather than "loosing."

It must be noted that the alterations, wittingly or unwittingly, subvert the traditional female imagery of the original text. Israel, mourning and in exile, is personified, capable of mourning, of loneliness, and of rejoicing. "Thy" Israel, the Israel of the Lord, subtly recalls the typology of Israel as the Bride of the Lord. The explicit reference to *birth* ("Emmanuel / Is born for thee, O Israel") is also female—and also stricken from the modern versions.

In the second stanza, Emmanuel as "Rod" is summoned. Such a rod—rather than a "strong Branch" (Lutheran and Episcopal) or "root" (Methodist)—has the power needed to "loose" the "captive." The "Rod" suggests justice and righteousness as well as natural growth "of Jesse's stem," the proper, natural correction of nature and history. In Neale's original, our liberation "from our enemies" is more historical-political and more biblical, more radical and less metaphorical, than the altered version, the Catholic excepted. Our revised captivity is strictly that of Satan, hell, and death. "Our enemies" may, in the original, be worldly oppressors (like the Egyptians and Babylonians) as well as Satan, hell, and the grave. Neale's original provided a more powerful, more biblical, and a more modern understanding of liberation than the revisions.

In the original second stanza we also note the direct, immediate vocabulary. "Satan's chains" are strong and immediate: we can almost hear them clanking. "The pit with all its pains," cast in monosyllabic words, is intentionally primitive and direct. The altered elegance of the Lutheran version is less striking and powerful: the simple "Free us" becomes "free Your own." "Satan's chains" become "Satan's tyranny," relatively abstract. "The pit with all its pains" becomes the "depths of hell." (The "vict'ry o'er the grave" simply doesn't belong here. The stanza is not about triumph or about death but about righteous liberation.)

The original third stanza invokes Emmanuel as "the true East." This is a bit odd, but Neale is a good enough poet that we should examine carefully what he's up to: *True* East is an absolute direction, in contrast to *eastward* or *easterly*. It also suggests truth as opposed to falsity and deception. Perfect direction and truth attach themselves to this image of the East. The east is also where we look for the dawn—"my soul waits" each day, of course, but especially at *East*er. The image of the East coming close ("draw nigh, draw nigh") is very fine, if a bit difficult. The morning sky, in contrast to the distant reaches of the immense and faraway night, seems close and friendly, a heavenly visitation.

This is a Latin translation by a poet steeped in classical literature, written for a public familiar with classical mythology. Accordingly, a word about the classical mythological understructure is in order: the dawn, as Aurora (or, alternatively, as our old friend the "morning star," who is Venus), is figured as female, beautiful and heavenly. Indeed, the stanza may be read as a female image of Emmanuel, nicely counterpoised to the "Rod of Jesse" with its macho function in a world of chains and pit and pains in the foregoing stanza. The divine female associations of the "East" find confirmation in the second line, where she "gives us comfort from on high." She is also strong enough to "drive away the shades of night, / And pierce the clouds, and bring us light." If the second stanza asks for and images forth liberation, the third sees Emmanuel as the great transcendent clarifier, the bringer of light. The lines are properly very visual and familiar.

The stanza generally substituted tries to avoid the difficulties of "East" by invoking, rather, the vaguer and less suggestive "blest Dayspring." The Dayspring cheers us up—a distinctly weak achievement compared to the transcendent illumination of the original. The new versions commonly reverse the order of ideas in lines 3 and 4 and replace active, finely envisioned lines with indirection: To "drive away the shades of night" suggests heroic energy defeating the combined evil of death (with "shades" as ghosts in hell) and natural darkness ("of night"). The original activities of "piercing" the clouds and "bringing" light are succinct and visual, summing up the function of the dawn-as-God-with-us. In contrast, to "disperse the gloomy clouds of night" is an imprecise activity, suggesting private melancholy and a poeticized dawn rather than the dawn as major combat. Similarly flawed, the new fourth line—"And death's dark shadows put to flight"—injects abstraction and complicated activity. What are "death's dark shadows" and where are they flying?

The fourth stanza petitions Emmanuel as "Key of the House of David" to open for us our heavenly home. One source of this imagery is certainly the Song of Solomon. If we read the stanza with reference to the Song, then the "House of David" is "my mother's House," loaded with erotic implications. (If we can avoid squeamishness, we might admit that the erotic implications are more powerful than the key as some sort of real estate mechanism.) Looking back, "thy Israel" was female, the heroic "Rod" was male, "the true East" was female. The "Key," to be inserted in the House, provides access to the domestic bliss of "our heavenly home." Such allegorical understanding of the Song of Songs is perfectly normal and traditional.

Images of the key and the home—whether rooted in the tradition of erotic religious metaphor or not—lead naturally to Emmanuel as protector and guardian who makes the way safe and keeps us from "the path that leads below." Keys offer security as well as penetration, providing safety and locking doors as well as opening them. These ideas seem somewhat garbled in the altered versions. The "Key of David" certainly makes less sense than the original "Key of the House of David." (What is a "key of David"?) To "open *wide* our heav'nly home" is strange because a key merely unlocks a door; it doesn't open it "wide"—the function, rather, of the hinges. The original *reopen* explains and reinforces the important domesticity of heaven-as-home.

The petition that Emmanuel "make safe the way that we must go" is immediate—perhaps recalling the threat of enemies (stanza 1) and the dangers of darkness (stanza 2) and anticipating the paths in which the shepherd leads the flock (stanza 5). The "path that leads below" recalls the pit. In contrast, the common change to "way that leads on high" is vague and disconnected from the narrative progress of the hymn. The "path to misery" is distressingly abstract since *misery* is a state of being rather than a place at the end of a path.

In the final stanza, Emmanuel is "Ruler and Lord." To *rule* is both to reign and to measure. The latter idea may recall the precision and right orientation of the "true East." Again we notice how the *closeness* of *draw nigh* plays its part: engagement, intimacy is desired, rather than the less exact "coming." This immediacy is reinforced by the Ruler as shepherd implicit in the second line. The fierceness of the Lord who drew nigh to Israel *as his flock* is mitigated. (The alteration of *flock* to *tribes* costs us this kindliness.) The law the Lord gave *as rule* or regulation recalls the "Ruler" of the first line. The concluding recollection of the historical event on Sinai leaves us with the prototype of the covenant, of God's transcendent concern and involvement in Israel's life.

We have noted how, in each stanza of Neale's original, the hymn switches from a petition to Emmanuel to a proclamation addressed to the faithful-as-Israel. This pattern is both dramatic (a matter of who is speaking to whom) and grammatical (as, in each stanza, imperative grammar cedes to declarative). The original order of stanzas is another important aspect of the shaping of Neale's hymn, what we might call its cosmic geography: In the first stanza, invoking Emmanuel, the desired action of the Lord is *lateral,* the loosing of the captive who is in "exile here." Here and there, in and out (*exile*), these happen on the horizontal axis. In the second stanza, we gradually move onto a vertical axis with the rod arising. The freeing from enemies and the unchaining suggest horizontal life's experience, but they assume transcendent, vertical meaning when our loosening is from *Satan's* chains and our freeing is from the *pit.*

In the third stanza, the nigh-drawing of the East itself becomes a dramatic part of what's happening. The East as a compass point is, by definition, horizontal-lateral. In Neale's stanza, however, it is forcibly wrenched out of the horizontal plane and becomes an emblem of transcendence, as that which comforts us from "on high" with power to dispel night, pierce clouds, and bring light. The third stanza of a five-stanza hymn, as it is central, may be expected to make a difference. Is it too much to suggest that the advent of Emmanuel is being dramatized here, in the heart of the poetry? Jesus, a baby born on the horizontal axis of historical experience, defies our logical expectations when he acts, as Redeemer, on the vertical axis—as Rod, as East, as Key—to loose and free and comfort. If this is what's happening, this is an extraordinary achievement in this genre of Christian poetry.

In the fourth stanza, freed by the agency of Emmanuel from captivity, from the pit, from the darkness, we can finally look upward to the house, the home, the way. (The worried glance back at "the path that leads below" is realistic.)

If this is the pattern, then the final stanza returns us to the horizontal frame of historical experience of the people of God. It is an experience of transcendence, of the vertical, however, on a mountain, where the Lord appeared from above. Having sung the hymn with understanding, we see how the experience of Israel, freed from captivity, looking down from Sinai, is paradigmatic of our own New Covenant.

The altered progression of altered stanzas is by no means so clear. It varies from hymnal to hymnal, but in the Lutheran text we proceed from the captive needing ransom (stanza 1) to the tribes on Sinai (stanza 2). (They don't ask for anything—a break in the pattern suitable for the finale but disruptive when the lines become the second stanza.) The upshot is that we end the revised hymn in heaven, in the old stanza 4, wanting to forget about earth. That's much less subtle and surely less suitable to the liturgical season anticipating the Incarnation than the original version.

Come, You Faithful, Raise the Strain

"Come, You Faithful" provides further demonstration that John Mason Neale was a fine poet who could seize and develop the materials of his ancient originals, molding them into exemplary congregational hymns. First published in the *Hymns of the Eastern Church* (1862), "Come, You Faithful" is based on the Greek original of John of Damascus, the first ode of the canon for St. Thomas Sunday, the first Sunday after Easter. The first three stanzas have us addressing the faithful, urging gladness, explaining it. We are, of course, these faithful, and we urge ourselves to rejoice and to understand as we proclaim the good news. We are also prepared, through the first three stanzas, for the final stanza, where, in the original, we address the risen Christ. All five hymnals include the hymn.

S. Thomas's Sunday

1. Come, ye faithful, raise the strain
      Of triumphant gladness!
   GOD hath brought His Israel
      Into joy from sadness:
   Loosed from Pharaoh's bitter yoke
      Jacob's sons and daughters;
   Led them with unmoistened foot
      Through the Red Sea waters.

2. 'Tis the Spring of souls to-day:
      CHRIST hath burst His prison;
   And from three days' sleep in death,
      As a sun, hath risen.
   All the winter of our sins,
      Long and dark, is flying
   From His Light, to Whom we give
      Laud and praise undying.

3. Now the Queen of Seasons, bright
      With the Day of Splendour,

With the royal Feast of feasts,
Comes its joy to render:
Comes to glad Jerusalem,
Who with true affection
Welcomes, in unwearied strains,
JESU's Resurrection.

4. Neither might the gates of death,
Nor the tomb's dark portal,
Nor the watchers, nor the seal,
Hold Thee as a mortal:
But to-day amidst the Twelve
Thou didst stand, bestowing
That Thy peace, which evermore
Passeth human knowing.

[Spurious fifth stanza]
Alleluia! Now we cry
To our King immortal,
Who, triumphant, burst the bars
Of the tomb's dark portal.
Come you faithful, raise the strain
Of triumphant gladness!
God has brought his Israel
Into joy from sadness!

In the first stanza, we urge ourselves to "raise the strain" of gladness. This peculiar expression seems to be an equivalent of "lift the song" or some such, but it signifies much more, providing a clue to what will follow. Most obviously, *raise* appropriately suggests the risen Lord. Less obviously, *raise* sounds like *raze* (to demolish) and the archaic *rase* (to erase). A *strain* is not only a song but also a wrenching, a tension, an element of *restrain* and *constrain*. The "razing" or "rasing" of "strain" in this second sense is the deliverance from misery, an important aspect of what's going on here and of what we celebrate on St. Thomas Sunday. Neale will collect on these secondary meanings in the coming lines.

In lines 3 and 4, the faithful—who are to be glad—are subtly identified with God's Israel: if *we celebrate* the deliverance of Israel, *we are* presumably Israel, brought into joy from sadness. "We" are thus the proclaimers (urging song), the rejoicers (urged to sing), and God's people (brought into joy). In line 5, the "loosening" from the "bitter yoke" recalls to mind the "rasing" of "strain" in the first line. (We "strained" under the yoke and rejoice at its "raising.") While the dramatic progress through the Red Sea retains its spectacular appeal in modern Exodus movies, the specificity of "unmoistened foot" is a surprisingly immediate detail.

The traditional—and typologically significant—reference to the Exodus is only the starting point, however, and it is in the first line of the second stanza that Neale metaphorically takes off. "'Tis the Spring of Souls to-day" is a marvelously packed line. Jacob's sons and daughters were "sprung" from bondage, their deliverance their "spring." The waters of the Red Sea make us think of the watery meaning of "Spring," perhaps of baptism. The Resurrection is the "Spring of souls" in a number of senses: it is the new epoch of history (season as historical division), and new life for individual souls (season of life). It is as well the *source* (as in "well-spring") of life and the *energy source* (like the mechanical spring that runs a watch or a wind-up toy). Certainly now Neale's pun in the first line is justified since springs deal with strain (and with loosing). When we proclaim, in the second line of the stanza, that "Christ hath *burst His prison*," the sheer bursting energy of the act fits nicely with the "Spring of souls" in its physical sense.

"Spring" also marks the end of winter as nature's "sleep in death" is at an end. Waking, however, belongs more exactly to the morning, to the rising Sun. Thus the Christ who bursts or springs from his prison is the sun/Son raised from the night of death. The multiple meanings all correlate exactly and work into the following lines. Here the winter which has passed is figured as the winter of our sins, "long and dark." (Note how both the winter and the sins are both long and dark.) Its end, with the Spring of the sun/Son, lets us celebrate the season, accommodating Christian symbolism to pagan springtime celebration of new life and light. This "winter" is personified in flight from "His Light," bringing to mind all the brilliant light imagery of the Easter vigil.

In the last two lines of the second stanza, the punctuation permits a rich complex of meaning. Most obviously, we give undying laud and praise to the Lord whose light has sent winter flying. But note how "His Light" is an agent, sufficiently personified to take on winter and send it flying. Read this way, the Light (who is Christ, the Light of the world) is the one "to Whom" we address our praise. The "undying" which most obviously modifies the laud and praise also attaches itself, by virtue of its position, to other items. The Lord is undying. The Light is undying. We who praise are undying. The action of the Resurrection is, pure and simple, *un*dying, the undoing of death. (The Lutheran alteration of *we give* to the passive construction *is given* sabotages a number of these suggestions. The Presbyterian elimination of half the hymn, including these lines, is grievous.) Such wealth of metaphorical option is characteristic of our best devotional poetry, from the so-called metaphysical poets of the seventeenth century, through Gerard Manley Hopkins, to the modern day.

In the third stanza, the Spring, with all its significance—new day, new life, life-source, energy-source, victor over death and sin—becomes a female personification, perhaps even the May queen, as Christ. The Queen of Seasons is springtime; the Day of Splendour is the Day of Our Lord. The "royal Feast of Feasts" is both the sacrament and the wedding banquet, prepared by the Lord for his bride, the Church, for Jerusalem, for Israel, whom he has delivered. The joy of deliverance in the first stanza has led to the laud and praise of redeemed nature. We proceed to the marriage feast, the coming of the Bridegroom to "glad Jerusalem." (This is *not*, as the Lutherans and Catholics would have it, simply "to gladden faithful hearts." Jerusalem is "glad Jerusalem" already. The word *glad* is an adjective here and *Jerusalem* is carefully defined through the associations that follow.)

The Queen of Seasons is particularly radiant ("bright") on this day. She attends the homecoming of the Lord, the Bridegroom, to Jerusalem. (The female personification of Jerusalem is inevitably the Bride of the Song of Songs.) The Bride is also the Church. *We* are the glad Bride. "Glad Jerusalem" recalls our own "triumphant gladness" from the first stanza. Her "true affection" is ours. Her "strains" recall the strain we urged the faithful to raise at the beginning of the hymn while the idea that they are "unwearied" recalls the richly suggestive "laud and praise undying" of the second stanza.

The achievement of the first three stanzas has been to orient us, as the people of God, to the Resurrection. This achievement is carefully marked by the resounding close of the third stanza (the Presbyterian conclusion). *We* are prepared to welcome the Resurrection. *We* are prepared, positioned to address Christus Victor.

The original final stanza, accordingly, begins with the acknowledgment of the specifics of the triumph: The "gates of death" which could not contain Jesus were, if you read your Dante or Milton, very specific, very spooky. The "dark portal" of the tomb, if you know your nineteenth-century paintings, is highly visual. The watchers and the seal, set to prevent deception, certify the Resurrection. We close the hymn with the disciples, witnesses to the living Lord, sharing in his benediction, "Thy peace, which evermore / Passeth human knowing." At the end we stand confirmed in our discipleship, witnesses of the Resurrection.

Almost needless to say, any alterations are apt to distort the fine progression of ideas and experience of this hymn. The Lutheran version of the fourth stanza, for example, refuses to allow our shift in address. We are no longer allowed our place among the Twelve, addressing Christ; we simply hear about what happened. This is a devotional loss. The new fifth stanza, appended by all but the Episcopalians, is a pastiche of rehashed lines, confusing the benediction that had closed down the hymn. The Alleluia is unnecessary. The "King" is gratuitous—the kingliness of Christ is not to the point at all. (Indeed, it suggests that the King is married to the Queen, who is the spring, a mythological disaster!) The bursting of the bars doesn't belong here. It prepared us to understand and participate in the events of St. Thomas Sunday but is past history now. Just so, the Lutheran return to Old Testament prototypical experience of Israel is anticlimactic at the end of what was once a very fine hymn, while the Catholic-Methodist Trinitarian praise is both larded with filler and beside the point.

VII: Other Nineteenth-Century Hymns in English

We would misrepresent the achievement of nineteenth-century hymnody if we failed to examine representative popular hymns. This is a category quite apart from either the poetic hymns of Heber or the translations from the Latin and the German. They come from many traditions, including the United States. These are not easy texts to handle. I find that, after a moment's review (although I haven't sung them for many years), I know these all by heart. The music clings tenaciously to the words. This should be a good test of our critical methodology.

All but the last of the four texts treated here share common characteristics. They mark the return to relatively simple metrics, perhaps an indication of their popular appeal (and, often, their design for children). Yet their contractions and vocabulary sound artificially "poetical" to modern ears, distancing us from the language. In these hymns the "I-as-singer" reflects on a life of sorrow and confusion rather than a life of suffering and sin. Internal struggle rather than external danger is the basic experience. Life here on earth is not very real. Most remarkably, the singer seems passively posed, postured, in prayer, at the foot of the Cross, at the breast of Jesus. The texts call to mind the religious paintings and prints of the era (paintings and prints which possibly affect our reading).

My Faith Looks Up to Thee

Ray Palmer's (1808–1887) "My Faith Looks Up to Thee" was first published in 1831. Lutherans, Episcopalians, Methodists, and Presbyterians have all included it, unaltered, in their hymnals.

My Faith Looks Up to Thee

1. My faith looks up to thee,
    Thou Lamb of Calvary,
        Savior divine!
    Now hear me while I pray,
    Take all my guilt away,
    Oh, let me from this day
        Be wholly thine!

2. May thy rich grace impart
    Strength to my fainting heart,
        My zeal inspire;
    As thou hast died for me,
    Oh, may my love to thee
    Pure, warm, and changeless be,
        A living fire!

3. While life's dark maze I tread
    And griefs around me spread,
        Be thou my guide;
    Bid darkness turn to day,
    Wipe sorrow's tears away,
    Nor let me ever stray
        From thee aside.

4. When ends life's transient dream,
    When death's cold, sullen stream
        Shall o'er me roll;
    Blest Savior, then, in love
    Fear and distrust remove;
    Oh, bear me safe above,
        A ransomed soul!

The first stanza orients the singer, who is down below, looking up to the "Lamb of Calvary," whom he or she addresses as "Savior Divine." This gives us a picture of who and where we are, positioned for prayer. The picture is complicated, however, by two items. That it is "my faith" which is looking up is a bit difficult, implying that it is through faith that we can see ("look up to") such things. The image, however, leaves the literalist wondering what "I" am doing while "my faith" is thus busy. It is likewise no simple, literalist idea that what "my faith" is looking at is not the Crucifixion—the body on the Cross—but rather the "Lamb of Calvary." The singer must know something about lambs and sacrifice and Calvary. Both the subject (the singer) and the object of contemplation (the crucified Lord, the "Savior Divine") are modified in order to enrich the meaning of what's going on. Such complications and assumptions at the beginning of a hymn either assume fairly sophisticated singers or indifference to complete understanding.

The orientation is a preparation to prayer, which is carefully prefaced with "Now hear me while I pray." (This seems more a signal to the singers, telling them what they're doing, than a notice to the Savior.) I pray for (1) the removal of my guilt which is forgiveness, and (2) dedication from now on. While we might expect these petitions to tell us where we're going in the following stanzas, this is not the case. They are prefatory rather than introductory. The hymn leaves the lamb, redemption, and the idea of dedication behind in the first stanza and proceeds to other petitions. Each of these refers back to the Passion story, but only after creating a little role, a little character, for the singer to play. The progression is more one of association than logical advance.

In the second stanza, the singer seems to pray for resuscitation. He or she is fainting with weakness, needing strength, needing the inspiration of zeal. *Inspire* suggests both a spiritual charge and blowing up or inflation. (The singer as a collapsed balloon comes to mind.) That this needed inspiration comes from "thy *rich* grace" is confusing. *Rich* may suggest either wealth or taste, and "rich grace" as food, giving strength to the "fainting heart," would be a nice eucharistic image. It is, however, subverted by the use of *impart* as the verb. We don't "impart" food. *Impart,* meaning to communicate or transmit, is more metaphorical.

The image of myself as a collapsed singer leads directly, if strangely, to the reference to the dead Savior ("As thou hast died for me"). Our weak, fainting, uninspired state seems to recall the crucifixion. Indeed the mystics, following Paul, speak thus of "Crucifixions" of the self. But this isn't really the point. Rather, my *gratitude* to the Lord for his death is to inspire my love. My petition, what I want, is love as "pure, warm, and changeless . . . a living fire." While there's nothing wrong with this desire for this love, we must note that the solution (pure, warm, changeless, living fire) doesn't match the problem, which was a perceived need for strength and inspiration. Purity, warmth, changelessness—these are very passive products of grace.

As my deathly state led me to recall the death of Jesus, so the living fire at the end of the second stanza leads me to think about life as a dark maze in the third, a maze from which "living fire" is absent. If I as singer was debilitated to the point of collapse in the second stanza, in the third I am mobile but lost. Life as a "dark maze" is despairing indeed, suggesting a hidden design with no clues for the singer as victim. (We may remember poor Cowper.) Moderns might even think of rats in a laboratory maze—the word *tread* even suggests their treadmills! Not only are we disoriented, without a clue, griefs are everywhere. So we pray "Be thou my guide." (The picture is a good example of hymn role-playing.)

Guidance is not all I ask, however. I also want the darkness (of life's maze) turned to day and sorrow's tears (at the griefs around me) wiped away. Actually, the first three lines were a setup, an introduction to these powerful biblical references. Our prayer that we never stray recalls the lost sheep and the petition for dedication from the first stanza.

While nice things are happening in the system of poetic and biblical language here, the overall pattern is moderately distressing. From the beginning of the hymn, "I" have been a very poor thing, weak, fainting, lost, sorrowful, in the dark. That's not bad, of course; I may well be such. But it's not just me. Life itself is wretched, so wretched that all I can ask for is purity, warmth, light, and comfort. Childlike, lamblike, I ask no agency, no activity. Life is unreal.

I have fainted, lost my way, wept bitterly and begged for zeal and guidance; yet, I find out in the fourth stanza (cut from the Episcopalian text) that all this trouble is basically unreal. Life is a "transient dream," ending in death. Actually, "death's cold, sullen stream," rolling over me, is the liveliest image in the hymn. That's poetically appropriate, of course, if life is but a dream from which we wake in death, but its essential otherworldliness, its cancellation of human agency or ethical activity, even love of neighbor or proclamation of the Gospel, is problematic for many Christians.

I only pray for the removal, in love, of fear and distrust *after death* (the fear and distrust that inform the picture of life in this hymn). My final ransomed safety "above" recalls my initial lowliness, how "my faith looks *up* to thee." We remember how, back in the first stanza, Palmer refused to call the crucified Jesus the crucified Jesus, how he gave us, rather, "Thou Lamb of Calvary, Savior divine." Could it be that this refusal fits with an other-worldly theological understanding that resists the real engagement of Jesus in real human life, turning rather toward heaven, toward death, toward release from the transient dream? At best, love in action in the world now—Jesus' or my own—is irrelevant here.

He Leadeth Me: Oh, Blessed Thought

Written by Joseph H. Gilmore (1834–1918), "He Leadeth Me" was first published in 1862. Retained by Lutherans and Methodists, it is a hymn response to Psalm 23.

He Leadeth Me: Oh, Blessed Thought

1. He leadeth me: oh, blessed thought!
   Oh, words with heav'nly comfort fraught!
   What-e'er I do, where-e'er I be,
   Still 'tis God's hand that leadeth me.
   > He leadeth me, he leadeth me,
   > By his own hand he leadeth me.
   > His faithful foll'wer I would be,
   > For by his hand he leadeth me.

2. Sometimes mid scenes of deepest gloom,
   Sometimes where Eden's bowers bloom,
   By waters calm, o'er troubled sea,
   Still 'tis God's hand that leadeth me. R.

3. Lord, I would clasp thy hand in mine,
   Nor ever murmur nor repine;
   Content, whatever lot I see,
   Since 'tis my God that leadeth me. R.

4. And when my task on earth is done,
   When by thy grace the vict'ry's won,
   E'en death's cold wave I will not flee,
   Since God through Jordan leadeth me. R.

The poet begins with exclamation, with general marveling at the familiar words, "He leadeth me." The process is meditative, signaled by the *ohs*: "oh, blessed thought" and "oh, words with heav'nly comfort fraught." Neither exclamation is very precise; "He leadeth me" is not really a "thought," at least not yet, and the idea of these words "fraught" with "heav'nly comfort" is a bit overdone. (Assuming we know that *fraught* is an archaic form of *laden* or *freighted*, is comfort a heavy weight, borne by words? The metaphor doesn't work.) But the blessings and the comfort will presumably be detailed in the lines that follow, so the first couplet is simply our starting point. The general summary of my possible activities and situations ("What-e'er I do, where-e'er I be") in which God's hand leads me is likewise introductory.

The basic idea of the psalm is not very difficult, and our response is very simple, very repetitive. The refrain repeats the declaration "He leadeth me" four times, picking up the idea from the last line of each stanza. This is incantatory, a sort of rote lesson out of a nineteenth-century primary classroom. The refrain emphasizes that it is "by his own hand" and my will to be "His faithful follower," but no connection between the leading of the Lord and my will to follow is made, no details or explanations are forthcoming. The picture in my mind is actually confused: if somebody leads me by the hand I walk beside him or her, not exactly following the leader.

The second stanza provides poetical-dramatical versions of biblical sites of the psalm *where* he leadeth me. This is a kind of cultural translation of the psalm material. I am led "mid scenes of deepest gloom" rather than the valley of death. I am led "where Eden's bowers bloom" rather than lying down in green pastures. I am led "by waters calm" and "o'er troubled sea" rather than the still waters. (*Still* is reserved, somewhat strangely, for God's hand.) Such cultural translation—as we shall observe in the nineteenth-century versions of earlier German hymnody—is quickly dated, and I doubt whether the gloomy scenes and Eden's bowers make much sense today. (Indeed, they may even sound hackneyed and trite.)

In the third stanza, the description of where I'm going cedes to my own will and feelings on the occasion. Again, we note the passivity of the singing self. I want to cling to God's hand ("I would clasp thy hand in mine"). This is a little odd: the metaphor of God's leading hand comes very clear as human and small, small enough for *me* to clasp in mine. (The Methodists have wisely substituted "I would place my hand in thine.") I would "not ever murmur or repine." (Such exertions are about all the vitiated singer seems capable of, and even they are what we *won't* do.) Finally,

I would be "content, whatever lot I see." (We don't actually "see" our "lot." It's cast, it's understood, it's given.) These partially formed ideas of human life and will should trouble us. Neither sin nor danger nor joy nor hope enter into the picture.

Life in "My Faith Looks Up to Thee" was a transient dream. Here, in the last stanza, it is supposed to be a "task" done and a "vict'ry won." We note, however, that there's been no actual task to perform and no battle to fight. Our efforts have been the minimal walk through a stylized landscape and silent contentment ("nor ever murmuring nor repining"). Neither vocation nor effort figure here. Even the submission to "Death's cold wave" (which "I will not flee") is unchallenging as it brings to mind little more than fears of children at the seaside—this despite the reference to crossing Jordan. Indeed, looking back, neither the heav'nly comfort nor my activities and situations in life have been explained at all. That's disappointing.

Beneath the Cross of Jesus

"Beneath the Cross of Jesus" by Elizabeth Clephane (1830–1869) was published in 1872. The hymn—again, sung only by Lutherans and Methodists—provides a familiar role for a weak and sorrowful singer, needing shelter, craving retreat. (Modern variant follows the original text in brackets.)

Beneath the Cross of Jesus

1. Beneath the cross of Jesus
     I [fain would/long to] take my stand;
   The shadow of a mighty rock
     Within a weary land,
   A home within [the/a] wilderness,
     A rest upon the way,
   From the burning of the noontide heat
     And [the] burdens of the day.

2. Upon the cross of Jesus,
     [Mine/My] eye at times can see
   The very dying form of one
     Who suffered there for me.
   And from my contrite heart, with tears,
     Two wonders I confess:
   The wonder[s] of [redeeming/his glorious] love
     And my unworthiness.

3. I take, O cross, [thy/your] shadow
     For my abiding place;
   I ask no other sunshine than
     The sunshine of his face;
   Content to let the world go by,
     To know no gain nor loss,
   My sinful self my only shame,
     My glory all[,] the cross.

We begin the first stanza with longing: I long to *be* beneath the Cross. Even though I sing that what I fain would do is "to take my stand," it doesn't seem that that's what I actually mean. To "take a stand" implies active assertion, but I really want comforting shelter rather than an opportunity for proclamation. In fact, the subject of the longing is itself problematic. What does it mean to long to be beneath the Cross? It might mean to wish one had been on Calvary, beneath the Cross, two millennia ago—clearly an impossibility, hence a suitable object for "longing" (although Jesus' disciples didn't find that "stand" comfortable). It might mean to want to be metaphorically "under the cross," presumably bearing one's own cross, heading toward one's own crucifixion. That's stretching things, but it's in keeping with the piety of crosses. It might suggest a grave-yard cross, of wood or stone. Pious paintings show women, especially women, beneath graveyard crosses—generally clinging or kneeling rather than standing. Nevertheless, the "stand" is troublesome in any of these readings. Many of us will be, in fact, buried "beneath the cross of Jesus," and the hymn seems to yearn for death.

In the balance of the first stanza, all these suggestions drift in and out. The dominant idea seems to be the singer as a homeless pilgrim, wearily crossing the wilderness in the heat of the day, carrying burdens. The cross is a huge rock, its shadow providing shelter. The land, like the singer, is weary. Darkness, coolness, cessation of activity are the objects of my longing for the cross.

In the second stanza, longing is no longer an issue: the Cross is simply there and I raise my eyes. (We have observed how crucifix hymns regularly move upward like this.) The corpus, the body, is only occasionally ("at times") or "dimly" visible. This suggests that the stone cross as shelter has been replaced by a vision of a crucifix—or that the crucified body is generally hidden from the singer who looks to the Cross for shelter. My modeled response as singer changes accordingly. Contrition and tears replace the pilgrim longing for shelter, and I am moved to confess the "two wonders." "Wonders" are usually pretty vague, hardly the substance of meaningful confession, and these are no exceptions: "the wonders of redeeming love" are nonspecific; the alternative "wonder of his glorious love" doesn't get us much beyond "Jesus loves me," while "my unworthiness," unexplained, is more lack of self-esteem than sin.

The third stanza briefly changes address. I have been singing to the world in general, reporting first on my longing for a position beneath the Cross and then on my intermittent vision of it and response to it. In the first two lines of the third stanza, I address the Cross itself. First "I take . . . your shadow / For my abiding place," somehow claiming what I had longed for in the first stanza. (The mechanism for this is not clear.) Then I commit myself to wanting only the "sunshine of his face." I have returned to the imagery of the first stanza in which the "burning of the noontide heat" was bad, an item in the unpleasant life of the burdened, homeless pilgrim in the wilderness. There I wanted cool darkness. Now I want that sheltered life to be illuminated by Jesus' face—never mind that the only image of Jesus has been the "very dying form." Never mind that this is a wish for obliteration, an indifference to the ordinary sunshine.

The properly oriented life of the last stanza is otherworldly. "Content to let the world go by," I am no longer a pilgrim en route. The world is rather en route and I am stationary, perhaps dead and buried, under a cross, noted by a passerby. I don't care about material things ("no gain nor loss"). I am reduced to two devout sentiments: shame for my sinful self and glory in the Cross. The last two lines are good, succinct verse. It's too bad that neither the sinful self nor any meaningful glory in the Cross have been explored.

O Savior, Precious Savior

The hymn "O Savior, Precious Savior" by Frances Ridley Havergal (1836–1879) was written in 1870. It stands apart from the other three selections by virtue of its plural voice ("we" sing), the relative energy of its devotional role modeling, and the relative complexity of its ideas. (Only the Lutherans saw fit to include this text.) The best clue to the progression of ideas is probably the sequence of last lines. The second word of the last line of the refrain changes from "*holy* Lord and King" to "*gracious* Lord and King" to "*glorious* Lord and King" to "*Savior* and our King." Indeed the emphasis in each stanza falls on the refrain and its modulations. We note how the first four lines of the first two stanzas are grammatically incomplete as sentences. They give us aspects of that "thee" whom we worship and are subordinate to our worship, blessing, praise, and confession. Only gradually, through the progress of the hymn, does our worship achieve coherence.

O Savior, Precious Savior

1. O Savior, precious Savior,
   Whom yet unseen we love;
   O name of might and favor,
   All other names above:
   We worship thee; we bless thee;
   To thee alone we sing;
   We praise thee and confess thee,
   Our holy Lord and King.

2. O Bringer of salvation,
   Who wondrously hast wrought,
   Thyself the revelation
   Of love beyond our thought:
   We worship thee; we bless thee;
   To thee alone we sing;
   We praise thee and confess thee,
   Our gracious Lord and King.

3. In thee all fullness dwelleth,
   All grace and pow'r divine;
   The glory that excelleth,
   O Son of God, is thine.
   We worship thee; we bless thee;
   To thee alone we sing;
   We praise thee and confess thee,
   Our glorious Lord and King.

4. Oh, grant the consummation
   Of this our song above,
   In endless adoration
   And everlasting love;
   Then shall we praise and bless thee
   Where perfect praises ring,
   And evermore confess thee,
   Our Savior and our King!

Precious is a wonderful word, signifying something of great value, something priceless. Its use as a kind of babytalk diminutive is perhaps thus unfortunate, as is the colloquial sarcasm of "there's precious little we can do." We have, however, watched colloquial usage become part of a hymn's design, watched it play off the primary meaning of a line. Frances Havergal, a linguist and poet, knew what she was doing. As it suggests value, *precious* is an economic image. When we stop to think about it, so is *Savior*, as it suggests "saving" (as in savings bank) as well as salvation. The placement of *precious* between two *Savior*s in a line beginning with the exclamatory *O* also taps into the intimacy of the loving use of *precious*. Obviously and most importantly, the Savior is precious to us, meaning simply very, very important. All three meanings work together.

That, in the second line, we love the precious Savior follows the intimate meaning of *precious*. That we love him "yet" means both "although" we haven't seen him and although we haven't seen him "yet." The future promise of seeing anticipates the second coming as well as the last stanza of the hymn, set in glory. We recall, of course, Jesus' blessings on those who have not seen and yet believe.

Indeed, the first stanza is all-concerned with the idea of *naming*, particularly the naming of the unseen that is precious and loved. We may recall Newton's consideration of the name of Jesus, but Newton was more concerned with the sound of the name in a believer's ear, with the effect. Havergal leads us in a different direction. We begin, in faith, with the name, the word, which was in the beginning. The preeminence of the name-word ("All other names above") calls forth our worship. This worship is of God *as holy*—immortal, invisible, ineffable, almighty. All these imponderables are implied in the text, which avoids abstraction, given the subject, to a remarkable extent. The experience is not particularly tangible, but that's appropriate for holiness, for our starting position.

In the second stanza, the last line signals us to look for an explanation of grace: we are worshiping the Lord as gracious. The Lord is accordingly identified as *active,* as "bringer of salvation" and as one who has "wrought" revelation. This is progress in understanding indeed: from mere name, however precious and holy, the Savior we are worshiping has developed. The "precious Savior" is not only word but also active deed. That the Savior reveals "love beyond our thought" gives us substantial evidence that transcends the limitations of intellect. This "revelation" counters the "yet unseen" of the preceding stanza. "Our gracious Lord" is thus active, evident, revealed love. The Savior is not only holy name.

In the third stanza, we work to get the idea of the Lord as glorious, whom we shall worship in the refrain. The idea is that, even more than active Savior, the Lord is the Son of God, therefore full of the comprehensiveness of God. Beyond the precious name, beyond bringing salvation and crafting the revelation of love, the Savior possesses "all grace and power divine." Now the sentences are complete grammatical units—as is appropriate to *fullness* and excellence. The glory of God, evident in Christ Jesus, makes it all work, both poetry and praise. If we glimpsed this idea back in the lines "O name of might and favor, / All other names above," now we understand. The "King" which concludes each stanza is realized.

If we have moved from name to act to divinity in the first three stanzas, in the conclusion we are able to pray, to petition the Savior. The song itself shall be completed in the future, when that which is "yet unseen" becomes visible. The future consummation and worship carries with it the ideas of eternity ("endless" and "everlasting" and "evermore") and perfection. The worship and blessing and praising and confession all culminate in a finale—both eschatological and poetic—in which we understand the substance of our own worship and the reality of "Our Savior and our King."

"O Savior, Precious Savior" seems a fitting conclusion to this little treatment of "other" nineteenth-century hymns, a reminder that hymns by women are not all passive, not all clinging, and that the desire for death as fulfillment is not necessarily morose! The plural voice of the Havergal hymn, a relief from the pathetic "I," suggests the source of the distinction, standard in hymnology, between objective ("we") hymns and subjective ("I") hymns. If, as our first three selections indicated, "I" hymns in the nineteenth century tended to model a role of self-absorption and vitiated otherworldliness, no wonder their subjectivity has been faulted. When, however, we contrast "My Faith Looks Up to Thee" with "When I Survey the Wondrous Cross," I think we can see that it's the devotional attitude of the nineteenth-century "I," not its voice, that disturbs us.

VIII:
Representative Translations of German Hymns

A t long last, in due course, we turn to look at several hymns we modern English-speaking singers regularly sing in translation from the German. While the originals belonged to an earlier age of Lutheran piety, the translations are, for the most part, very much the work of Victorian England and modern America. We shall begin with a hymn by the Victorian Catherine Winkworth and proceed to a contemporary translation by Gracia Grindal. Then we return to the nineteenth century with Robert Bridges's lovely "Ah! Holy Jesus" and conclude with a modern treatment of "A Mighty Fortress Is Our God." This alternation should allow us to compare and contrast older and newer versions.

The exact treatment of the hymns we know from modern hymnals *as translations* demands heavy scholarship indeed. Original German texts are compared to original versions of translations and then compared to modern versions of translations. This is important work, especially for Lutheran hymnology, this examination of the legitimacy of translations of canonical Lutheran hymnody. I attempted such a study of Catherine Winkworth's "Jesu, Priceless Treasure," a study published, with a new translation, in the *Lutheran Quarterly* (Summer 1988). The results were distressing, as they indicated that Winkworth was unappreciative of both the wealth of imagery and the piety of the original. Other hymns are not so badly garbled. Setting aside my own suspicion of the authenticity of translations, in these pages we shall look simply at the translations as first they appeared in English and as they have been altered for modern use. These are, after all, the hymns as most of us know and sing them.

Jesus, Priceless Treasure

A translation of "Jesu meine Freude" by Johann Franck (1618–1677), the original text of "To the Savior" ("Jesus, Priceless Treasure"), comes from Catherine Winkworth's (1827–1878) *Christian Singers of Germany*. Lutherans, Methodists, and Presbyterians sing versions of this translation.

To The Savior

1. Jesus, priceless treasure,
    Source of purest pleasure,
        Truest friend to me!
    Long my heart hath panted,
    Till it well-nigh fainted,
        Thirsting after Thee!
    Thine I am, O spotless Lamb!
    I will suffer nought to hide Thee,
        Ask for nought beside Thee.

2. In Thine arm I rest me,
   Foes who would molest me
       Cannot reach me here;
   Though the earth be shaking,
   Every heart be quaking,
       Jesus calms my fear;
   Sin and hell in conflict fell
   With their heaviest storms assail me.
       Jesus will not fail me.

3. Satan I defy thee;
   Death, I need not fly thee;
       Fear, I bid thee cease!
   Rage, O world, thy noises
   Cannot drown our voices
       Singing still of peace;
   For God's power guards every hour,
   Earth and all the depths adore Him.
       Silent bow before Him.

4. Wealth, I will not heed thee,
   Wherefore should I need thee,
       Jesus is my joy!
   Honours, ye may glisten,
   But I will not listen,
       Ye the soul destroy!
   Want or loss or shame or cross
   Ne'er to leave my Lord shall move me,
       Since He deigns to love me.

5. Farewell, thou who choosest
   Earth, and heaven refusest,
       Thou wilt tempt in vain;
   Farewell, sins, nor blind me,
   Get ye far behind me,
       Come not forth again;

Past your hour, O pomp and power;
Godless life, thy bonds I sever,
    Farewell now for ever!

6. Hence all thoughts of sadness,
    For the Lord of gladness,
        Jesus, enters in!
    Those who love the Father,
    Though the storms may gather,
        Still have peace within;
    Yea, whate'er I here must bear
    Still in Thee lies purest pleasure,
        Jesus, priceless treasure!

Several formal items immediately catch the critical eye. First, there is the remarkable meter. With the long stanzas and the complicated sequence of line lengths (6-6-5-6-6-5-7-8-6 syllables) we have come a long, intricate way from the simple psalm meters of Watts. The rhymes are no less demanding of the translator than the metrics. Each stanza requires three pairs of so-called "feminine rhymes." (In a feminine rhyme, two syllables rhyme, with the accent falling on the penultimate syllable: treasure-pleasure; panted-fainted; hide thee-[be]side thee.) Finally, the seventh line of each stanza is divided in two rhyming halves: "Thine I *am*, O spotless *Lamb*," "Sin and *hell* in conflict *fell*," and so on. Such patterning presents a double challenge to the translator, who must meet its demands without letting the effort show. (The effort shows whenever the only explanation for a particular word choice is that it rhymes.)

We are next struck by the severity of the cutting. When half the stanzas are eliminated from all three hymnal versions, we may assume that either the original was chaotic or that our version is a sort of *Readers' Digest* edition. (While church musicians commonly complain that no modern congregation will sing more than three verses of anything, it seems to me that a hymnal should remind its users that their text is incomplete, that the gaps in the sense are not the poor poet's fault.)

The first stanza addresses Jesus, invoking three metaphors in the first three lines: Jesus as priceless *treasure,* as *source* of pleasure, and as *truest friend.* The three are fine traditional comparisons but not particularly compatible with one another. They stand in isolation from one another. In lines 4 and 5, I the singer report on my intense longing for Jesus. The implicit metaphor is Jesus as drink, after which—as after a cooling stream—I—or my heart, as the hart—pant and thirst. It's yet another idea, however, unless the idea of Jesus as *source* of pleasure makes pleasure sufficiently liquid to explain this thirst. (Yes, we may expect such coherence.) The seventh line is a single declarative sentence, an affirmation of belonging. We note, however, that the Jesus as a treasure (which I, by implication, possess) of the first line jars oddly with Jesus as my owner ("Thine I am") here. Further confusion comes from this agent as a "spotless Lamb." While the individual images are unexceptionable, they fail to lock in place.

The final two lines of the first stanza express the exemplary reaction to such a realization of belonging: nothing else obtrudes. I the singer *will not allow* anything to get in the way, to "hide Thee." The expression *suffer* as "tolerate" is not really familiar or easy to follow, and we don't know, at least not yet, what things might be hiding Jesus or why. The last line has its charm, the delight of double meaning: we want nothing "beside Thee" in the sense of more than or other than Jesus. The line also means that next to or "beside" Jesus, we have no other wants. The Lamb of line 7, however, complicates this exemplary reaction. Am *I* looking for a lost or hiding lamb, who is Jesus? (That's an odd twist on the parable.) Are we "beside" the Lamb?

The metaphorical confusion carries over into the following stanza. The arm (Methodist "arms") of Jesus in which we rest is a vestige of the powerful divine love language of the German original which Winkworth suppressed. In the original, my pleasure in Jesus is much more romantic and makes much more sense. Here the arm quickly turns from love to protection from nameless "Foes who would molest me" (Presbyterian "oppress me"). The arm removes us from the world of enemies. In the fourth line we change address, no longer speaking *to* Jesus but rather *about* him and his role in our lives. In times of natural disaster (earthquake) and general panic (heartquake), "Jesus calms my fear." This retreat is looking very much like the popular position of the passive, vitiated singer of the last chapter.

In the last three lines of the stanza a wild battle is underway, a good instance of hymn drama. Sin and hell, personified, wage war, attacking the singer with "their heaviest storms." In all this wild melee, "Jesus will not fail me."

The Lutheran alteration of "heaviest storms"—suggesting really terrible weather and recalling the violence in nature of the shaking earth from line 4—to "bitter storms" indicates the general trend of the alterations to this hymn, a general trend that we do well to recognize in modern versions of sixteenth- and seventeenth-century German hymns: exterior, large world experience is psychologized, interiorized, spiritualized. It's as if we in the modern age no longer needed to cope with the big fears, with evil loose in the world. We, rather, have our heartaches and private agonies to deal with. Metaphors are regularly revised in this direction, stanzas cut to make the originals less public, less active.

Note how the picture of passive hiding in the arm of Jesus (a weak version of the original Lover Jesus) has led us to the dramatic cosmic conflict, the high adventure. This is the setup for the defiant, assertive central stanzas of the hymn, stanzas 3 and 4. When they are cut out, as indeed they are cut by all the modern versions, the hymn misses it's own point. Here we find our role.

The third stanza models our defiance of Satan, whom "I" address in yet another shift of address. Satan, Death, and Fear are giant evil forms from whom we assert our independence. The protection and calming, unfailing support of Jesus have enabled this action. These are expressions of our strength. Such defiance is further explained and dramatized in lines 4 through 6, where the raging world is put in its place. The idea of drowning (the world "cannot drown our voices") recalls the storms of the previous stanza with the story of Jesus saving the disciples on the sea. The song of peace we sing is, ironically, a challenge, like the hymns of the apostle in prison. That we sing "still" is a pun—both "yet" and "quietly."

While there's lots of activity here—defying, flying, ceasing, raging, noisemaking, drowning, singing—we note that the activity generally belongs to the world and the evil powers. *I*, passively, will not fly, bid cessation, sing of peace. In the last three lines, the guarding power of God recalls the arm of Jesus in which "I rest me." When all earth and "the depths" adore him, the metaphorical waters which threatened to drown our voices are controlled, silenced in worship. As in the popular nineteenth-century hymns we surveyed, activity is inimical to spirituality.

Continuing to shape our response, the fourth stanza directs us to ignore Wealth—personified and dismissed as unnecessary. We recall Jesus as treasure. Honours are accused of promoting our spiritual ruin as well, although here the poetry falters badly. (They "glisten" and we are tempted to "listen," which indeed rhymes, but we normally *see* what glistens and *listen* to what speaks.) We'd like to know a bit more about how "Ye the soul destroy," another instance of the *activeness* of evil contrasted with the *passivity* of good. At the end of stanza 4 the address shifts yet again, from the contemptible Wealth and Honours to the general world. The expression becomes so dense it is virtually impenetrable.

The fifth stanza has us bid farewell to the wrongheaded people who opt for this world rather than heaven (yet another shift of address). These people tempt us. Then we bid farewell to sins that, variously, blind us and lead us. The use of *farewell* is obviously unfortunate as it implies a blessing! We ask that our friends and family "fare well" when we are separated. We certainly shouldn't bless the damned worldlings, sins, or the godless life. In the sixth line the awkward picture of sins "coming forth" or not "coming forth" is hard to justify, but the confusion gets worse and worse as we address "pomp and power" (as "past your hour") and "godless life" with its bonds.

As Winkworth originally intended it, the final stanza has me tell myself to cheer up and receive the Lord of gladness (lines 1–3), has me remind myself that inner peace will sustain me through gathering storms, and has me assure myself that, despite the burdens of life, perfect pleasure lies in Jesus, the priceless treasure. As the hymn has been cut, these activities and happenings are unrelated to one another. What does Jesus' entrance have to do with the storms or with my burdens?

To my mind, Winkworth's original is neither a particularly satisfying nor a very helpful hymn. The incompletely developed, everchanging metaphors, the shifting address, and the tension between the wild metaphysical dramatics and the passivity required of the soul are confusing. The role modeling of a believer who pants and thirsts and rests and retires from the world, clinging to inner peace, does not seem to me to speak to our age. Perhaps if the role were more constructive, the confusion might be allowed. If the metaphors were organized, perhaps the role might come clear. The combination, however, is overwhelming.

Perhaps the editors who cut and reassembled this hymn were attempting to bring order to chaos. If so, their results are unfortunate. When we skip the lines shaping our defiance of death and sin and voicing our rejection of worldly values, the substance of stanzas 3 through 5, we are left with a version of interior, fearful, passive faith even weaker than the original translation. Neither English version retains any of the power of the German original.

Out of the Depths I Cry to You

Given the difficult formal and devotional demands of "Jesu meine Freude," it is not surprising that no retranslation was commissioned for our modern hymnals. It is, however, odd that Winkworth's text of "Out of the Depths" was replaced by a modern rendering in both the Lutheran and the Methodist hymnals.[*] It's much better—as an accurate translation and as a hymn—than "Jesus, Priceless Treasure." (Perhaps the nineteenth-century tendencies toward interiorization especially suited the "depths" of the subject.) Composed by Gracia Grindal (b. 1943), the new "imitation" of the classic German rendition of Psalm 130 ("Aus tiefer Not") forces our attention to new issues.

The familiarity of the psalm and its cry make the translator's job difficult, recalling for us what must have been Watts's experience in his day as he recast the psalms in then-contemporary language with reference to then-contemporary Christian experience. (He called his psalms "imitations.") The critical reader's job is also difficult, complicated by the familiarity of the psalm, the Winkworth version, and the German original.

---

[*] Episcopalians use a late seventeenth-century psalm paraphrase, while Presbyterians adapt the Richard Massie version.

When are archaic expressions simple and appropriate deference to the psalm, and when are they inadequate communication, incompatible with the idea of contemporary translation? How much familiarity with Christian doctrine and devotion may the hymn presume in its singers? How free is the "imitator" of a text to introduce new ideas and angles before he or she loses the right to call a translation a translation? "Out of the Depths" provokes a whole series of such troubling questions.

Out of the Depths I Cry to You

1. Out of the depths I cry to you;
        O Father, hear me calling.
    Incline your ear to my distress
        In spite of my rebelling.
    Do not regard my sinful deeds.
    Send me the grace my spirit needs;
        Without it I am nothing.

2. All things you send are full of grace;
        You crown our lives with favor.
    All our good works are done in vain
        Without our Lord and Savior.
    We praise the God who gives us faith
    And saves us from the grip of death;
        Our lives are in his keeping.

3. It is in God that we shall hope,
        And not in our own merit.
    We rest our fears in his good Word
        And trust his Holy Spirit.
    His promise keeps us strong and sure;
    We trust the holy signature
        Inscribed upon our temples.

4. My soul is waiting for the Lord
   As one who longs for morning;
   No watcher waits with greater hope
   Than I for his returning.
   I hope as Israel in the Lord;
   He sends redemption through his Word.
   We praise him for his mercy.

© 1978, *Lutheran Book of Worship*

The Grindal hymn, like the psalm, begins with a suggestive archaism. But we may well ask what depths we cry out of? We are clearly *down* here, God *up* there, whence he may *incline* his ear. Is this vertical understanding appropriate to a modern hymn? (It is interesting to observe that the German text avoids such a suggestion. The singer cries "aus tiefer Noth," out of deep distress. Deep is a modifier, not "the depths" or the abyss itself.) The modernization "I cry to thee" to "I cry to you," is, it seems, misleading if the recasting of the text imposes an archaic, vertical cosmology.

But perhaps this is too literal and these are metaphorical depths, the depths of despair or grief or anxiety, and singers naturally know this. Perhaps we can justify the address to God as "Father" in the second line on similar grounds of familiarity. Again, the "new" version of the hymn introduces an archaism absent from the original. The German text addresses "Herr Gott" (Lord God), not "Father." We may well wonder what we're doing *adding* paternal ideas for God when they are unnecessary! (Methodists correct this to "O Lord, now hear.") The problem goes beyond feminism, however: God may well be cried to as "Father" when the role we are playing is that of rebellious or prodigal child. That isn't the case here at all, however. Indeed, the father-child image complicates the picture terribly. Calling on the Father is a new item, a new metaphor for our attitude toward God. Here it recalls Jesus' cry from the Cross, a recollection that is less than helpful in this context, as we shall see.

Is it, in fact, "me calling" that I want God to hear? I think not. I want God to hear *what* I call, not the activity, which the participle conveys. Again, in the third line, the image is confused: God might listen ("incline [God's] ear" if, indeed, that's what this strange expression means) to a verbal communication but not "to my distress." Distress is a state, a condition, not something articulate. "My distress" is actually abstract, especially in contrast to the simple "to me" (as what God is asked to hear) of the original German. That God should do so "in spite" is neither nice nor gracious. Of course that isn't what's meant, but the expression *in spite of* carries the idea of spite with it. (Poetry works that way, either to our advantage or to our distress.)

My rebelling is not explained. The idea, moreover, does not work with the series of "my" activities. Are we crying, calling, distressed, *and* rebelling? Was Jesus, *who cried to the Father* from the Cross, rebelling? (Grindal has brought Jesus into the picture.) The item *my rebelling* is incompatible with the other imagery as it stands. *My rebelling* is also imprecise and demands an almost Miltonic appreciation of rebellion. (The original of "my rebelling" is the more direct and immediate experience of sin and injustice.) Just so, the petition of the next line that God not "regard my sinful deeds" is challenging. We seem to have shifted ground, moved on to another topic, from God's hearing to God's vision, without a transition. If the "depths" out of which I cry have to do with rebellion and sin rather than grief and anxiety and suffering, we need a link, an explanation. *Regard* seems unnecessarily archaic. What is its exact meaning here? Does *my sinful deeds* simply mean "my sins"? (I think it is a roundabout poeticization—sounding pretty and filling up the syllables, but indirect.)

The critical singer can only wonder just what the hymn is having me do and why, and just what I want the God whom I address to do. Why, in the penultimate line of the first stanza, do I ask for "the grace my spirit needs" rather than the grace *I* need? Must I have a spirit, whatever that is, to sing this hymn with conviction? As a Christian, however humble, I acknowledge *my* need for grace. I'm not sure about my spirit, however. The last line is most logically troublesome, however. Without the grace my spirit needs, "I am nothing." But what does this mean? If you haven't sent it, *as I have just sung*, then I am nothing. But then who's been crying, calling, singing, praying? The conviction of one's nothingness, however biblical, needs explanation.

In the second stanza, we acknowledge that "All things you send are full of grace." This certainly sounds biblical, but in a hymn we may properly resist vague generalities. What *things* do you send and how may they be imagined as "full of grace"? With its crowning and favor, the next line is impossibly obscure and archaic. What do "crowned lives" and such "favor" mean? The declaration that "All our good works are done in vain without our Lord and Savior" compounds quasi-biblical abstraction with theological imprecision. "Good works" is technical terminology, here locked into the passive voice (when "our works are done" rather than "we work"). If they are vain, the hymn should help us understand how this is so, either by developing the implicit fine idea of vanity or by explaining the relationship or lack thereof to "our Lord and Savior." If, to turn back to the last line of the preceding stanza, "I am nothing" without God's grace, then my good works must be manifestations of God's grace rather than vain, no? Since the implication has been that *nothing* is done "without our Lord and Savior," how can our good works be done without him?

The address has shifted between the second and third lines of the second stanza, from address to God to a general report. We seem to have left the depths as well, and our original cry has become praise (line 4). The God we praise is one "who gives us faith" (line 5). Again, the hymn makes sweeping assumptions about the theological sophistication of singers and their tolerance for one- or two-line statements, strung together but unrelated to one another, interspersed with archaic, biblical-sounding citation. Poetic figures don't quite work either. God gives us faith and "saves us from the grip of death." This implies a personification of death, a venerable idea of a gripping Grim Reaper. Unfortunately, this personification of death is the antecedent of *his* in the following line, suggesting that our lives are in *Death's* keeping, not the point at all. Actually, even without the confusion about the antecedent, the line "Our lives are in his keeping" is virtually unintelligible. It seems to attempt a sort of Middle English *keep* as stronghold, but the word doesn't work.

The first line of the third stanza manages to illustrate two poetic sins: filler words packing the line and inverted word order. "It is in God that we shall hope" simply means "We hope in God." In the third line, to "rest our fears in his good Word" seems an unnecessarily obscure expression. "His promise keeps us strong and sure" is, for all its resonance, not a very clear declaration. Moreover, neither our weakness ("he keeps us strong") nor our uncertainty ("and sure") have been at issue. The business about "the holy signature" escapes me entirely. It may be an unfortunate reference to baptism—although in baptism the sign of the cross is commonly drawn (not inscribed) on the forehead (not the temples). Its status as a "signature" is doubtful.

Suddenly the first five lines of the fourth stanza are perfectly clear and direct, eloquently phrased, a fine example, in short, of hymn poetry. The role of the singer as one of the watchers is clearly defined and carefully sustained over five lines, accessible to the humblest singer. The penultimate line, however, stumbles in confusion. Our waiting, longing, hoping is so succinct that we want more than the abstract theological declaration, "He sends redemption through his Word." We wait for, long for, hope for something much more meaningful than this, *for the Lord himself,* in the biblical language paraphrased here. The mercy, certainly, for which we praise him, must be more a matter of immediate and tangible experience than this "redemption through his Word."

Reading this hymn in this chapter, we have slipped out of the nineteenth century for a moment into a modern world of religious language in crisis. There seem to be few resources for hymn poets aside from, on the one hand, the hollow abstractions of theological language, language constructed to scientific specifications and (ironically) distorted by Germanisms, and on the other hand, a sort of modern approximation of the poetry of the King James Bible. Modern hymn poets, finally, share in the general cultural suspicion of poetry, but this is to anticipate our final chapters.

Ah, Holy Jesus

While "Jesus, Priceless Treasure" represents a nineteenth-century approach to the divine love hymn of the German Pietist tradition, and "Out of the Depths" is a twentieth-century sort of psalm paraphrase (loosely following the German original), "Ah, Holy Jesus" marks the effort of a fine poet to write an exemplary hymn meditation on the Crucifixion. We do well to recall Watts's Passion hymns "Alas! And Did My Savior Bleed" and

"When I Survey the Wond'rous Cross." Watts's Passion hymns sprang from the same Baroque sensibility. Indeed, they were written within eighty years of the Johann Heermann (1585–1647) original, "Herzliebster Jesu."

In her *Hymnal Companion to the Lutheran Book of Worship* (Philadelphia: Fortress Press, 1981), Marilyn Stulken reports the general consensus that the work of Heermann "marks the transition from the objective hymns of the Reformation to the more subjective hymns of the following period" (223). This is that same "subjectivity" which I think has been so seriously misunderstood: the "I" of such a hymn is a construct, an example, a role model we are made to follow, shaping perfect faith. It is no more subjective or egotistical than other kinds of hymnody. It does suggest the need for forceful manipulation of the response of singers, whose spontaneous devotion is not trustworthy.

Robert Bridges's five stanzas follow the general lines of the fourteen-stanza original. Our text is from the *Yattendon Hymns* (1897), a collection which has provided a trove for compilers of hymnals (including our four sample Protestant collections) although it was never intended for church use.

Ah, Holy Jesu

1. Ah, holy Jesu, how hast thou offended,
   That man to judge thee hath in hate pretended?
   By foes derided, by thine own rejected,
   O most afflicted.

2. Who was the guilty? Who brought this upon thee?
   Alas, my treason, Jesu, hath undone thee.
   'Twas I, Lord Jesu, I it was denied thee:
   I crucified thee.

3. Lo, the good Shepherd for the sheep is offer'd:
   The slave hath sinnéd, and the Son hath suffer'd:
   For man's atonement, while he nothing heedeth,
   God intercedeth.

4. For me, kind Jesu, was thy incarnation,
   Thy mortal sorrow, and thy life's oblation:
   Thy death of anguish and thy bitter passion,
       For my salvation.

5. Therefore, kind Jesu, since I cannot pay thee,
   I do adore thee, and will ever pray thee
   Think on thy pity and thy love unswerving,
       Not my deserving.

First, certain formal observations: Each stanza of "Ah, Holy Jesus" is built of three long, eleven-syllable lines, followed by a short, concluding line. The five conclusions thus provide a sort of outline of the hymn response. Scanning them, we note how we begin with the *pity* of "O most afflicted"; proceed to acknowledgment of *our own involvement* ("I crucified thee"); then to recognition of *God's intercession;* then the realization of *its purpose;* and, finally, to *our unworthiness.* This is a fine use of form to reflect perfect, appropriate progression of realization and response.

The rhymes are also noteworthy. They are all feminine, that is two-syllable rhymes, the second a weak beat: *offended-pretended; rejected-afflicted; upon thee-undone thee; denied thee-crucified thee;* and so on. Managing these in English is so difficult that this challenge alone almost explains the frequent inadequacy of English translations of German hymns. (Eleven-syllable lines that begin with a weak beat—as a good reflective hymn should—would naturally conclude with a weak beat, even if the music didn't insist, which, of course, it does.)

We begin, in the first stanza, with the general pity anyone might feel before the crucified Lord and the questions that pity inspires. The initial *Ah* is expressive, signaling intimacy. It meets the challenge of the German *herzliebster.* ("Most-dear-to-my-heart" works in German but not in English.) Our address to Jesus as "holy Jesu" balances and restrains the intimacy. (Note how, after the intercession of stanza 3, "kind Jesu" replaces "holy Jesu," a change appropriate to our growing appreciation of what's going on.)

Observing Jesus on the Cross, we question: What have you done to deserve this? "How hast thou offended" takes that basic idea and adds layers of suggestion and association. The idea of "offending" includes common offense in interpersonal relationships—a friend might ask "how have I offended you?" It includes sins—we traditionally asked God's forgiveness of "our offenses" when we confessed together. It includes crimes—from misdemeanors to capital offenses. Observing the Crucifixion, perhaps for the moment pretending ignorance, we naturally ask what Jesus' offense was.

The question as to offense introduces the essential role reversal of redemption. That Jesus has not offended but that "man" has presumed to play the judge is the substance of the second line. Here the twisting of the syntax, the abnormal arrangement of words, suggests the abnormality of what's going on. Bridges writes "That man to judge thee hath in hate pretended." Normal order would be "That man in hate hath pretended to judge thee." The distortion of the words appropriately reflects the distortion of the act (as well as a bit of German word order). *Pretended* connects back, through its rhyme, to *offended.* The real offense was the pretense to judgment. To "pretend" suggests presumption, fiction, confusion, all these things. (The comma originally separating lines 1 and 2 was necessary, preventing the suggestion that "thou [Jesus] offended that man." The Methodist *we* for *man* is premature—"we" don't accept blame yet. The Presbyterian line, "That mortal judgment has on you descended," loses both the pretense and, as "judgment" descends, human agency.)

The third line treats *agency,* the real nature of who's doing what to whom. Jesus as the *object* is stressed by the constructions "by foes derided, by thy own rejected." In contrast to Jesus' hypothetical status as offender, we find him the victim of others' acts (of the foes and of his own people). *Foes* and *thine own* are intentionally vague, however, since we haven't clarified any of this yet in our devotional progression. We have only come as far as the recognition that Jesus is "O most afflicted," the victim.

The second stanza marks the investigation into this offense and the trial. We begin with the question "Who was the guilty?" The expression "who brought this upon thee?" carefully casts the Crucifixion as a burdening victimization by an agent, identified in the next line. But we (except the

Methodists, who changed the pronoun in the previous stanza) don't jump forward eagerly to confess. Rather, we hesitate, as is only natural. In the second line we sneak up on the subject: We have remarked elsewhere how *alas* seems a bit contrived (as in "Alas! And Did My Savior Bleed"), a bit distant. We don't take blame immediately but initially deflect it onto an abstraction: "Alas, my treason, Jesu, hath undone thee." Treason is indeed a crime, but it takes a bit of thought to feel the guilt. That my treason "hath *undone* thee" is a very rich idea. Such "undoing" most colloquially simply means "gotten you in trouble." (Drink was his undoing.) To be "*un*done" is also to be destroyed, unmade, ruined. Zippers and clothing are also undone. However we read it, it takes the idea of Jesus as object, as afflicted victim, that has been building up and begins to acknowledge our blame.

In the third line we recognize and forthrightly confess our undeniable involvement in this affliction. Up to now the emphasis had lain on "thou . . . thee . . . thine own . . . upon thee." Now, after "my treason" is acknowledged, we shift to "'Twas I . . . I it was . . . I crucified." Our initial indignation has ceded to terrible realization, direct and heightened. The triple expression is progressive: *'Twas I* is (like Watts's *Alas*) poeticized and artificial expression. *I it was* is a bit less so, but still inverted and not yet colloquial. *I crucified thee* is direct, unmitigated, undistorted, uncompromising.

The third stanza of five is formally central. (Presbyterians omit it.) Here Bridges gives us a *Lo,* which we recognize as the signal for a demonstration. Rather than a usual hymn tableau, however, he presents us with two familiar analogies, both instances of the unusual, extraordinary nature of what is happening in the Crucifixion. (We remember the distortion of line 2, where the language reflected the same extraordinary upset in the nature of things.) The unaccountable figures are the Shepherd offered for the sheep and the Son suffering for the sins of the slave. Note how the complexities of the atonement are conveyed in simple, accessible, biblical analogies rather than in arcane abstraction. The hymn speaks in parables, laying open the significance of the Passion. The immediacy of these illustrations permits and balances the theological terminology of *atonement* and *intercedeth.* Our "unheeding" indifference is all the more reprehensible after we have seen the Shepherd offered and the suffering Son.

In the fourth stanza we turn to "*kind* Jesu" (Presbyterian *dear*). *Kind* means nice and sweet but also "of our kind," an appropriate name for one whose "incarnation" was "for me." Incarnate, Jesus joined human*kind,* in *kind*ness and compassion. That incarnation entailed four items, two per line: *mortal* sorrow and *life's* oblation (line 2), *death* of anguish and *bitter* passion (line 3). The "offered" and the "suffered" of stanza 3 are explained, in terms of the Incarnation, here in stanza 4. *Oblation* is doubtless the most troublesome word in the hymn—meaning both offering and sacrifice and bread and wine. It hardly seems worth its own obscurity—unless, perhaps, a word we only struggle to understand suggests our struggling to understand what it was "kind Jesu" did with his life. Certainly and clearly, it was "for my salvation."

In the final stanza, the singer is led through the recommended, exemplary reaction to this new understanding and its consequence. Now, in the first line of the last stanza, *kind,* in conjunction with the idea of payment, suggests that it is "paying [Jesu] in kind" which is not possible. The expression, the idea of paying Jesus, recalls the pretense of judgment back at the beginning. It's equally absurd. Perhaps payment also recalls the treason of Judas as well as our Sunday church offering. "I adore thee" because it's all I *can* do but also *because* I cannot pay thee, such is the relationship, transcending the normal world of orderly economic exchange. *Since* carries both meanings. I "will ever pray thee" means I will pray unceasingly *to* thee but also that I will "pray thee" in the sense of *petition you to* do what follows in the next line—"Think on thy pity and thy love unswerving, not my deserving." Alternatively and also, *I* will pray *that he will* think on thy (his) pity and thy (his) love and not on my deserving.*

Such multiple, simultaneous meanings enrich a hymn. So do related patterns, collections of meanings. Human actions are, throughout the text, cast in negative terms. Humanity pretends and judges in hate, derides, rejects, afflicts, undoes, denies, and crucifies. Jesus is the victim, the recipient, derided, rejected, afflicted, undone, denied, crucified, offered. In stanza 4, the actions of Jesus are cast as nouns rather than verbs: incarna-

---

* The Presbyterian changes—*kind* to *dear* and *pray thee* to *praise you*—betray the poetry and the sense: I pray (or petition) you to think of *your own* pity and love.

tion, sorrow, oblation, anguish, passion. Items in a subtle grammatical drama, the parts of speech are part of the meaning of a rich and suggestive text.

A Mighty Fortress Is Our God

In his *Dictionary of Hymnology*, John Julian provides a synopsis of the plot of Martin Luther's (1483–1546) "A Mighty Fortress." He writes how "In st. i. we see our stronghold and its besiegers; in st. ii. our weakness, our Saviour's power and might; in st. iii. the vanity of the Prince of this World; in st. iv. whatever earthly goods we lose we have our true treasure in heaven." The synopsis is faulty and misses a good deal, suggesting that no less an authority than Julian sometimes has read carelessly. Julian also wisely observed that Psalm 46 is more a motto than a text for the hymn, which forms its own images.

Episcopalians, Methodists, and Presbyterians retain the nineteenth-century translation by Frederick Henry Hedge (1805–1890). Catholics substitute Michael A. Perry's (b. 1942) contemporary version. Our basic text is the Lutheran "hymnal version," a remarkable kind of anonymous poetry, presumably generated in committee.

A Mighty Fortress Is Our God

1. A mighty fortress is our God,
      A sword and shield victorious;
   He breaks the cruel oppressor's rod
      And wins salvation glorious.
         The old evil foe,
         Sworn to work us woe,
         With dread craft and might
      He arms himself to fight.
   On earth he has no equal.

2. No strength of ours can match his might!
    We would be lost, rejected.
But now a champion comes to fight,
    Whom God himself elected.
            Ask who this may be:
            Lord of hosts is he!
            Jesus Christ, our Lord,
        God's only Son, adored.
He holds the field victorious.

3. Though hordes of devils fill the land
        All threat'ning to devour us,
We tremble not, unmoved we stand;
        They cannot overpow'r us.
            This world's prince may rage,
            In fierce war engage.
            He is doomed to fail;
        God's judgment must prevail!
One little word subdues him.

4. God's Word forever shall abide,
        No thanks to foes, who fear it;
For God himself fights by our side
        With weapons of the Spirit.
            If they take our house,
            Goods, fame, child, or spouse,
            Wrench our life away,
            They cannot win the day.
The Kingdom's ours forever!

© 1978, *Lutheran Book of Worship*

Many things are going on at once in this classic Reformation text. We note first that its process is conventional, by which we mean that singers are led through an expression of exemplary faith, articulating confident attitudes that they may or may not feel at the moment, learning by singing. I think that a second kind of pedagogy, also familiar, is also evident. We are handed puzzling or provoking images which we only half understand, which are meant to raise questions. Such questions are then answered by the hymn, clarifying and consolidating our position. This is a classic Christian humanist intellectual engagement that calls us to active participation, active response. The hymn is also conventionally "spectacular," by which I mean that it has entertainment value, engaging us with its dramatic action, action reminiscent of *Star Wars* and *Dungeons and Dragons* and, certainly, the chivalric romances, familiar to Luther and revived in the nineteenth century, that were the prototypes for modern adventure films and other fantasies.

The first line, so familiar that it's hard to examine it objectively, is actually a challenge. We may well ask *how* God can be a fortress, which is, after all, a building, an old sort of building few of us have ever seen? We manage most *human* metaphors easily, but *architectural* metaphors are difficult. Metaphors help us by comparing strange and difficult items with familiar, easy things. For most singers, God is probably more familiar than a fortress. I actually think the metaphor belongs to the pedagogy. It is *meant* to provoke resistance, to make us ask "how" God can be a building. We should resist. The puzzle will then be solved.

If we stop to think about it, which we should, the second line, which gives us God as "a sword and shield victorious," is at least as problematic. With our contemporary interest in metaphorical theology, what do we make of God as weapon? Is this hopelessly archaic? Is our attachment to the hymn simply nostalgia?

Lines 3 and 4 move us on from these troublesome noun metaphors to related verb metaphors for God's activity. These settle more easily in our imaginations. God "breaks" the rod of oppression and "wins" salvation. The sword and shield seem suddenly justified by this activity of liberation from oppression. Indeed, God as liberator is more imaginatively accessible than God as protector, so Luther began there. Or perhaps God as liberator is more accessible to the modern political imagination than God as protector—a rather feudal idea.

In four lines we have five military metaphors. The careful metaphorical setup introduces the spectacle, which we are to observe with the basic metaphors of fortress and sword and shield, breaking and winning, in mind. The action is that of single combat, familiar from medieval romances. The idiom, the choice of words, is monosyllabic, recalling older, Germanic forms of English with words like *foe* (contrast *enemy*) and *woe* (contrast *misery*) and *dread* (contrast *distress*). Our old evil antagonist, our sworn enemy, powerful and crafty, "arms himself to fight." Of course his "arms" recall that "sword and shield victorious" of the second line, the arms of the ultimate conqueror of this foe. As the stanza concludes, however, we're not at the point of the divine victory yet. "On earth he has no equal" resoundingly affirms the power of *Satan.* Although I have a hunch that most singers think they're ascribing such power ("on earth he has no equal") to God, that's an unfortunate misreading. It's not surprising, given the general failure of contemporary men and women to acknowledge the power of Satan, but it's unfortunate for the sense of the hymn.

In the second stanza, the line "No strength of ours can match his might" continues our acknowledgment of the power of Satan and our helplessness before him. Again, I'm not sure how singers read this. Such power is necessary to the drama. We are to tremble in our metaphorical boots at the prospect of Satanic victory. This threat is, it seems to me, inadequately conveyed in the line "We would be lost, rejected." The vanquished are neither lost nor rejected but rather dominated and overwhelmed.

In the third line, the mysterious champion enters. This is a scene right out of the lore of knights in shining armor, engaged in contests of strength and valor. We announce that he is God's chosen hero but sustain the dramatic suspense when we rhetorically "Ask who this may be," this anonymous knight. The next three lines identify him—again in something like the medieval formula used on such occasions—by military reputation ("Lord of hosts"), by his feudal position in relationship to us ("Jesus Christ *our Lord*"), by genealogy ("God's only Son, adored"). The final announcement of his triumph on "the field" of battle echoes the "victorious" of the second line of the first stanza. So the imagery of God as sword and shield, those disturbing weapon metaphors, have been explained and dramatized in the first half of the hymn. (To understand how the champion Jesus' battlefield victory is a victory of God's sword and shield, we could use a bit of information about the election of champions by kings, but never mind.)

In the third stanza the antagonist is different—no longer the single foe, taken on by God's champion. Rather "hordes of devils fill the land / All threatening to devour us." The new analogy is to barbarian invasion, to a swarm of cannibalistic antagonists. Here the fortress idea begins to come clear, the idea of protection, of holding firm against invasion. The expression "Unmoved we stand" and our confidence that "They cannot overpow'r us" belong to this new configuration.

The figure of the raging prince of this world is, it seems to me, intentionally ambiguous. He is Satan, of course, who, we have sung, is unequaled on earth (stanza 1, line 9), but also a powerful mortal enemy. We are oppressed people, but oppressed by a fierce power who is "doomed to fail." The hymn seems to stagger here, confused by its own ambiguity. "God's judgment must prevail" is a new idea: we haven't been talking or thinking about *judgment* or any justice metaphor at all. It doesn't belong. Then, even worse, "One little word subdues him" is grammatically off. *Him* seems to be God, who isn't subdued at all! (Pronouns normally refer to the most recent suitable noun, which here seems to be God.) Stanza 3, for all its confusion, leaves us with a good question: *What* "little word subdues him"? I guess we have to let this question puzzle us. That's how we progress.

The finale, the last stanza, unfortunately suggests that the word is "God's Word," which, *fortress-like* "forever shall abide." While the "little word" is not the same as "God's Word," the ear hears no difference. We're slowly getting the fortress idea, although the littleness of the word is no help at all to our identification of *Word* and *fortress*. "No thanks to foes who fear it" is, it seems to me, unnecessarily obscure. Who are these foes, and why are they foes? If they are foes, how could we even expect to thank them ("no thanks") or credit them with sustaining the word? What is the purpose of the line? (We deserve an explanation in a hymn in which foes are so important.)

The following image of God fighting by our side "with weapons of the Spirit" seems to put the Trinitarian seal of approval on the whole battle scene. We had been picturing Christ as the champion, as the sword and shield of God. Now God is fighting with us, with weapons provided by the Spirit. However Trinitarian, this is extremely confusing. Suddenly we're in danger—both poetry and people.

It really matters who those foes were and how they feared the word, because they're the ones threatening to seize all the dear items of the next line. The indefiniteness of the foes leaves us with a vague sense of paranoia—unless we live under violent oppression and an application is obvious. Here in the last stanza we're into a new fight. As the single combat between Satan and God's champion changed to the defensive battle against invading devils and this world's raging prince, so the third battle is the very real prospect of martyrdom. I think that we have difficulty claiming that experience with any conviction, that almost any application of such imagery to mainstream, English-speaking Christian life is a dangerous distortion. But perhaps such a political critique is out of place here.

In the last two lines, where we return to the championship idea, the "winning of the day," the Kingdom that is ours is presumably not of this world. (Julian got that right.) Satan is preeminent on earth. Our confidence is basically a confidence in the final victory. This suggests that the hymn as we have it reneges on its own military-political imagery.

I think that formal features of the hymn can help explain its difficulty, its lack of clear progression. We first note that each stanza is grammatically divided into two parts by the periods that follow each fourth line. This division is confirmed by the metrics and the rhymes of each stanza, which we can diagram as follows (with breves as unaccented syllables, macrons as accented):

PATTERN OF ACCENTS	NUMBER OF SYLLABLES	RHYME PATTERN
˘ ¯ ˘ ¯ ˘ ¯ ˘ ¯	8	*a*
˘ ¯ ˘ ¯ ˘ ¯ ˘	7	*b*
˘ ¯ ˘ ¯ ˘ ¯ ˘ ¯	8	*a*
˘ ¯ ˘ ¯ ˘ ¯ ˘	7	*b*
˘ ¯ ¯ ˘ ¯ (or ¯ ˘ ¯ ˘ ¯)	5	*c*
¯ ˘ ¯ ˘ ¯ (or ˘ ¯ ¯ ˘ ¯)	5	*c*
˘ ¯ ¯ ˘ ¯ (or ¯ ˘ ¯ ˘ ¯)	5	*d*
˘ ¯ ˘ ¯ ¯	6	*d*
˘ ¯ ˘ ¯ ˘ ¯ ˘	7	*e*

The first four lines of each stanza are very regular, standard even. Accented and unaccented syllables alternate perfectly over the course of thirty syllables (8+7+8+7). The four lines are knit together with interlocking rhymes. Skimming back through the hymn, reading only the first four lines of each stanza, we can see that these lines and their progression are very clear, unexceptionably even. (It's just possible that these are the only lines anybody ever takes seriously.) The last five lines are, in contrast, highly irregular (a contrast evident in the music). The pattern of accents in the three five-syllable lines varies from stanza to stanza. The last line stands alone, resonant but unconnected by rhyme.

Following these formal clues, we note the breaks in the stanzas. In stanza 1, the five suggestive *but largely incompatible* military metaphors disappear after the first four lines as we turn to the "old evil foe." In this second half, the metrical irregularities, following the tidy alternation of accents of the first half, illustrate the satanic confusion and distortion. The language is bent and twisted. The two halves of the stanza are antagonistic to one another, just as Satan is antagonistic to God.

The first half of the second stanza returns to the formal regularity of 8787/*abab* but continues the discussion of Satan and our dire situation. Rhyming words also tie this half stanza into the preceding half stanza—the words *might* and *fight* are repeated. The initial military metaphors have disappeared in the background and we are preoccupied with Satan. The entrance of the champion intrudes—only in this stanza is there a period after the second line of the stanza. Again the break after line 4 is significant as we turn to provoke the question "Ask who this may be" and to answer it. The second half of the stanza is preoccupied with recognition or identification. Here the irregular meter sounds conversational and puzzled, a nice effect.

The first half of the third stanza claims exemplary confidence before the hordes of devils—another radical shift in subject. The second half switches again, from hordes back to Satan (or his political representative). By the last two lines of the stanza, the strain of all these scene shifts is beginning to tell. (Remember how neither "God's judgment" nor the "little" word are integrated.)

This confusion only gets worse, the judgment ignored, the word abstracted, in the first half of the last stanza. The foes are unidentifiable. "God fights by our side" attempts but fails to recall Jesus as champion or the prevailing of God's judgment. The pictures don't fit together. The weapons of the Spirit are new and unidentifiable, out of place in what's left of the adventure story.

The most damaging break happens, however, in the last stanza. Here we switch from guaranteed victory, with God at our side, to the imagined oppressors who will probably succeed in victimizing us. That's a real jolt. That they "cannot win the day" and that "The Kingdom's ours forever" violates all the metaphorical achievement of the hymn, however fragmented. Evidently God is only a metaphorical fortress and his sword and shield don't accomplish much at all in this world. The cruel oppressor's rod will only be broken at the end of time. The battle with Satan is irrelevant. The hordes of devils really can overpower us.

We're lost in a metaphorical tangle. Military metaphors are immediate and worldly, incompatible with this sort of otherworldliness. The more clearly we imagine fortresses and swords and shields and oppression and single combat and invasion, the more committed we are to the coming of the Kingdom now.

All hymns are in some measure "sacred" texts, loaded with the pious good intentions of their authors, the weight of scriptural reference, and the experience of generations of singers. "A Mighty Fortress" is especially sacred in this sense of the word—the original author especially authoritative and the Lutheran experience of the hymn especially meaningful. It is just that author and that Reformation experience, however, that urge us to examine and to question texts and traditions, to insist on meaning and on the insufficiency of human excellence. Perhaps the best test of the reformation heritage is our willingness to read "A Mighty Fortress" critically and to work to clarify its expression.

IX: Third World/ Liberation and Experimental Hymnody

erhaps now, as we move toward "modern" hymnody, the time is ripe for a reminder that this little collection of hymn studies is not a history of hymnody. We have not presumed to survey the vast and varied tradition of congregational song and to draw sweeping conclusions about the rise and development of Christian hymnody. Such a book would have to command almost unimaginable resources, including biblical scholarship, comparative and international denominational and literary history, and carefully coordinated musical and textual study. (I would like to think that it would also require some method for the close reading of texts that is not unlike the method practiced in these pages.)

Our selection of writers and of hymn texts for examination in these pages has, accordingly, neither pretended to be representative nor random. If one claimed that selected texts were somehow representative, one would claim familiarity with the whole body of hymnody and an a priori historical model which those texts had been chosen to illustrate. Such familiarity is impracticable, and such a historical model is at best premature. Random selection, at the other extreme, might prevent the unavoidable bias that attends on conscious choice of favorite or particularly familiar hymns. In this case it might defend me from the suggestion (which I anticipate) that I have "stacked the deck," choosing texts to reinforce my own opinions about Watts or Wesley, Heber or Neale, or eighteenth- or nineteenth-century hymns. It would, one suspects, also yield many careful analyses of texts that are hardly worth the trouble, either to perform or to read. We want texts that matter.

Random selection would also confuse or belie the historical perspectives and the theoretical expectations that inevitably accompany any textual study. Hymns, like other poems, may be presumed to have grown and developed in gradually changing contexts. These contexts, as we reconstruct them imaginatively, in retrospect, are artificial, biased, the products of limited human brains. They are, however, necessary. We cannot read meaningfully without a sense of context. Hymn writers knew the hymns of their predecessors and shared access to common models. We can usually only imagine how this tradition and these conventions affected a given writer. Meanwhile, the Christian community's sense of its own devotional and educational needs changes over the years. This sense is variously explained and understood. In the absence of a definitive and authoritative history, a perfectly objective reading of these developments is neither possible nor desirable. Comparisons and relative judgments, passing insights, useful perspectives—these lesser offerings, however modest, are worthy still.

As it has not been completely sifted by the selections and reselections of hymnal compilers—and given its astounding international diversity—modern hymnody in English is an even wider and wilder field than traditional hymnody. Judgments and historical perspectives, categorization and classification become more and more difficult, less and less authoritative.

Neither the Christianity nor the poetics of hymns seem quite as certain as they might have been in a former age. As we approach the field with our relative and modest kind of history, however, certain modern patterns seem to suggest themselves. In these last two chapters we shall survey three of these trends. The first of these is a *third-world* or *liberation trend* that often reaches across old ethnic and geographic lines to encompass the global community of Christians. Of course, this means new kinds of hymn texts, new understandings of hymnody, and radical challenges to translators, singers, and church musicians. Political problems accompany the liberation idea, problems as to motive and understanding of *liberation* song, problems as old as colonialism and as fresh as our capacity for solidarity. The second trend is toward *experimental hymnody*. These hymns invent new models or adapt other kinds of song to hymn use. We shall treat sample modern versions of the third trend, toward *traditional hymnody*, in our final chapter. These are hymns doing what hymns have always done but in language and with reference to an experience that is distinctly our own.

Third-World and Liberation Hymnody

The Christian world is a large and diverse community and it behooves modern Christians to learn as much about the Christian experience of people unlike themselves as possible. We have many good motives for such education: We may be motivated by love and concern, by brotherhood and sisterhood, or by the simple, human fascination with what's different. Or we may be motivated by the need to hear the Gospel, to be preached to. Certainly the profound faith of Bishop Desmond Tutu or of Bishop Romero inspires and moves us. Or we may know our need to be led out of our own parochialism, our little private world of Christian people just like us. We may realize how we tend, without such consciousness, to take possession of Christianity, to define and limit it to our own culture. Most of us want to resist the sort of Christian colonialism that has marred too much mission effort in the past.

Contemporary third-world and liberation hymnody in our churches seems intended, in the first instance, to widen our horizons, to break us out of parochialism. It is, further, something of a political act. The motives we scanned above are largely political. They imply that we need liberation from our own white, powerful, colonial perspective. They imply that we can somehow express our solidarity with Mandela and Bishop Tutu and the victims of oppression in Central America when we sing African and Hispanic hymnody. Hymnody can raise our consciousness. Besides, solidarity feels good!

We do well, however, to acknowledge that this is a new item in the pedagogy of hymnody. We have seen how hymn texts through the centuries have sought to clarify and direct our devotional attitudes and responses. Hymn writers have taken common states of mind, common understandings, and developed and expressed them. When we sing hymns from other traditions with a view toward consciousness-raising, we are adding another kind of education.

Several dangers attend this adventure. The first is that we will think that having fun in the sun in Mexico is the same thing as experiencing solidarity. Another is that we will somehow oversimplify the Christian experience of the other tradition, reducing it to a delightful primitivity. A different danger is that we will expropriate the experience of other people through our solidarity. Can prosperous, white, American people sing meaningfully about our deliverance from slavery? Or does such singing insult the martyrdom of millions of African-Americans? To what extent must hymns match our experience?

I have suggested in the foregoing chapters that traditional English-language hymnody is in bad shape. We don't pay careful attention to the words we sing, and when we do we often find that they don't really make much sense. Perhaps a final danger of third-world and liberation hymnody is the *apparent* simplicity of otherness, unburdened as it seems to be by tradition, naively divorced, as packaged, from its own rich, indigenous cultural context. There's often a sheer pleasant relief in simple, intelligible texts and stirring music. The careful translation and adaptation, the processing for contemporary American consumption, rarely shows. To this extent, third-world and liberation hymnody, however politically correct, may represent a dangerous double retreat—from both respectful engagement with the complexity of otherness and from our own tradition with all its unreasonable demands.

Alabaré, Alabaré

The Mexican song "Alabaré, Alabaré" is found in the Lutheran collection of *Songs of the People* (Minneapolis: Augsburg Publishing House, 1986). It simply illustrates the insufficiency of good intentions.

Alabaré, Alabaré

Refrain:
> Alabaré, Alabaré,
> Alabaré, Alabaré,
> Alabaré a mi Señor.
> Alabaré, Alabaré,
> Alabaré, Alabaré,
> Alabaré a mi Señor.

1. Worthy is Christ, the lamb who was slain,
   Whose blood set us free from our sins.
   Power and riches and wisdom and strength
   And honor and blessing shall be his.

2. John saw the number of all those redeemed,
   And all were singing praises to the Lord.
   Thousands were praying, ten thousands rejoicing,
   And all were singing praises to the Lord.

This traditional song takes us back to our earlier discussion of repeated alleluias and Reginald Heber's triple holies. The weight of the hymn falls on the ten *Alabarés* (Praise!) of the refrain. They're fun. And in fact we are praising Christ in Glory, just as we were in "Holy, Holy, Holy," but with Latin rhythm. The text of the first stanza paraphrases the song of the saints in the Book of Revelation, the saints whose parts we're playing. In the second stanza we step back, modify the address, and explain a bit about what's going on.

The simple fun of the hymn is seductive. Half of it—the refrain—is incantatory, unintelligibly so for singers who don't know Spanish. The other half is paraphrased Scripture and simple story. There's no progress, no demand for understanding, no pain, and no gain.

So what do we *mean* when we sing a song so unlike the normative hymns of our tradition? I hope we don't mean to have a Spanish devotional experience! The Spanish-Hispanic tradition is a rich mine of profound spirituality. I hope we don't mean to frolic with the natives, enjoying the pious pleasures of simple people! That doesn't fit with our educational and political understanding at all. I only hope better motives than any I can imagine are out there. Such adventures in third-world and liberation hymnody present questions of motive. The idea, after all, was to raise consciousness.

Come, Let Us Eat

The hymn "Come, Let Us Eat" by Billema Kwillia (b. c. 1925) was translated from the Loma language of Liberia by Margaret D. Miller (b. 1927). The fourth stanza was added by Gilbert E. Doan (b. 1930). Although it is insistently repetitive, the text—included in the Lutheran and Episcopal hymnals—conforms much more closely than "Alabaré" to our traditional expectations:

Come, Let Us Eat

1. Come, let us eat, for now the feast is spread,   (repeat)
   Our Lord's body let us take together.   (repeat)

2. Come, let us drink, for now the wine is poured,   (repeat)
   Jesus' blood poured let us drink together.   (repeat)

3. In his presence now we meet and rest,   (repeat)
   In the presence of the Lord we gather.   (repeat)

4. Rise, then, to spread abroad God's mighty Word, (repeat)
   Jesus risen will bring in the Kingdom. (repeat)

St. 1–3: © The Lutheran World Federation
St. 4: © 1972, *Contemporary Worship 4*

Examining "Come, Let Us Eat," we remember the cruel facts of hymn translation: the English version has to work on its own terms, making good sense and doing its proper job. We may recall the challenges of feminine German rhymes and extraordinary metrical forms. Accuracy only mattered in such a context of formal demands. Certainly African hymnody presents its own unique formal problems—although charting accuracy is simply beyond our reach here. In this hymn, for instance, we note how the repetition of every line demands wording that can take the strain. (The Episcopalian version has a "Leader" sing each line and "All" repeat it, a fine pedagogy reminiscent of the lining out of English hymn texts by the parish clerk back before hymn books.) At the same time, such two-line stanzas seem to call for an exact tension between the two lines, a balance, even a dialectic. There's no room for imprecision or fumbling around.

If the first "balance" is implicit in the repetition and the second a balance between the two lines of each stanza, the third is a metaphorical balance, contained in the images. This hymn seems to understand itself as *elemental*, both in the sense of basic and of presenting the sacramental elements for our understanding. We find a perfect balance between common, human, colloquial experience and expression and the extraordinary. The language is richly allusive. The expression "Come, let us eat," for example, is *almost* prosaic, but not quite. Two or three times a day I may say to my family, "Come, let's eat." The slight touch of formality, the spelling out of the contraction, is the only language difference here as we, as believers, invite one another to the table. But that's not all we do. We also suggest a motive. We are to come *because* ("for") *at this moment* ("now") the feast is spread. It's the appropriate thing to do. But there's more still. *For now* also means it won't be there forever. It's only spread "for now." That makes the invitation urgent. Finally, *for now* suggests the blessedness of the moment: the feast is spread for *now*, for the *present time*, for its benefit and pleasure. The present moment rather than some future time is sanctified. That's a good sacramental point.

Especially in such a colloquial text, the idea of a "feast" suggests celebrative social eating, like our Thanksgiving or Christmas feast, "a real spread" at a family reunion. At the same time the word *feast* is unusual enough to recall dozens of biblical feasts and celebrations of the people of God. We probably catch as well a bit of African feasting, saved from the fun-in-the-sun dangers of exoticism by the rich suggestions of universal feasting.

"Come, let us eat" is perfectly balanced with "Come, let us take" in the second line. The juxtaposition forces us to recall the familiar words of institution, "take . . . eat." Again, the seemingly commonplace, upon reflection, is holy, is sacramental. The word *spread* also attaches its meaning to the next words, *Our Lord's body.* This happens because of simple word order and because the second line comments upon, transforms, the first. "The feast" that "is spread" *is* "Our Lord's body." The body is both *spread* on the table, the feast we eat, and *spread* on the Cross in crucifixion. The second line elevates the commonplace, simply confessing that what was initially ordinary—the feast, spread—is so no longer.

In this context, to "take together" the Lord's body means several things at once. It is a fine synonym for *communion,* less Latinate and unfamiliar. (I don't think it would work generally, but in this context it's just fine.) We "take" the Lord's body "together" in community, with our fellow Christians. We also "take" the body "together" with the feast: however it happens, we confess that when we eat this feast we eat that body, the two "*to*gether." To "take together" is also a countermovement to "spread." "Spreading" is offering, proffering, setting forth; "taking together" is collection, gathering, receiving. Such giving and receiving are essential aspects of what's going on.

The amazing first stanza has set the pattern which the following stanzas work from. Again, only such wealth of meaning permits the repetitions. We need to repeat, to reflect, to let the words connect and speak to each other. The repetitions are far from mindless.

In the second stanza, similar things are happening. "Come, let's drink" is also colloquial, even more joltingly so, again restrained. "The wine is poured" links up even more solidly with "Jesus' blood poured" than the spreading with the body in the prior stanza, confirming the pattern of juxta-position and interrelationship between the lines. "Jesus' blood poured" seems to take on a little life of its own as an independent action, as in "Jesus' blood poured from his side," a suitable distraction. The "drinking together," as it recalls the "taking together," is highly suggestive. Because of the established pattern, the stanzas echo, reecho, and elaborate on what we have already sung. The meanings accrue and multiply.

The third stanza is clearly the natural conclusion of the hymn, as the language reaches the height of allusion. "In his presence" is, of course, "the real presence." It is also the simple presence of the Lord. We also come together *in his presents* (a good, traditional pun), which are the bread and wine, the body and blood. Through the hymn, we have come to understand the urgency of "now" as motive for our coming (a sort of cook's impatience with the family's delay in coming to the table as well as a reminder of the "nowness" of the sacramental moment). Can we also appreciate "his presence" as "his presents" as these exact, present moments, these accumulated "nows" when we come?

Now "we *meet*" picks up the threads of "take together" and "drink together." When we "meet," we are together—*at* meat (or dinner), as is "*meet*, right and salutary" (or appropriate). To *meet* others is a social act. "Now we meet" also rhymes with "let us eat," suggesting the balance of communion-as-gathering and communion-as-eating (or meat). That we "meet and rest" requires a bit of reflection. To "rest" is to obtain peace, the achievement of benediction. We "rest" in peace. To rest is also to remain and, indeed, we remain in our meeting, in communion. We also want ordi-nary rest, perhaps a good nap, after an extraordinary feast. The last line is a fitting conclusion: The "presence of the Lord" *is* our rest, what we are left with, our remainder. We "rest in the presence of the Lord." The *we gather* recalls the *together*s and the meeting, the together-coming of communion that, like a dance movement, balances the out-spreading of the feast and the body of the Lord.

I think we can understand the motive for adding a fourth stanza, a felt need to urge each other to "go in peace and serve the Lord" after the sacrament, to fit the hymn to a standard devotional pattern. This fourth stanza, however, as it fails to appreciate the richness of the original and its natural conclusion, just doesn't belong. It introduces new actions, new directions. The verbs of the first three stanzas have been so carefully managed, so carefully balanced between the colloquial, commonplace, and the powerfully suggestive, so carefully juxtaposed. In the new fourth stanza, *Rise* just isn't of the same order as *come, let us, take, drink. Then* forces the direction of the hymn into a now-now-now-then pattern, imposing an unnecessary second conclusion. "To spread" God's Word abroad, as it recalls the spread of the feast and the body, confuses the act, already carrying the weight of the sacramental presence. Neither the mightiness of God's Word nor the one-liner summary of proclamation are to the point of the hymn. Their poetic idiom is heavy-handed and completely out of keeping with the delicacy and depth of the first three stanzas.

Lift Every Voice and Sing

Among the most stirring of modern liberation anthems, James W. Johnson's (1871–1938) "Lift Every Voice and Sing" recalls the violent past of African Americans, celebrates the achievement of freedom, and looks to a future of both faith and liberty. Remarkably, all five of our sample hymnals include almost exactly the same text. (In this and subsequent texts, variants are placed in brackets.)

Lift Every Voice and Sing

1. Lift every voice and sing
   Till earth and heaven ring,
   Ring with the harmonies of liberty.
   Let our rejoicing rise
   High as the list'ning skies;
   Let it resound loud as the rolling seas.
   Sing a song full of the faith that the dark past has taught us;
   Sing a song full of the hope that the present has brought us;
   Facing the rising sun
   Of our new day begun,
   Let us march on, till victory is won.

2. Stony the road we trod,
   Bitter the chast'ning rod,
   Felt in the days when hope unborn had died;
   Yet with a steady beat,
   Have not our weary feet
   Come to the place for which our parents [people, fathers]
       sighed?
   We have come over a way that with tears has been watered;
   We have come, treading our path through the blood of the
       slaughtered,
   Out from the gloomy past,
   Till now we stand at last
   Where the white gleam of our bright star is cast.

3. God of our weary years,
   God of our silent tears,
   Thou who hast brought us thus far on the way;
   Thou who hast by thy might
   Led us into the light;
   Keep us forever in the path, we pray.
   Lest our feet stray from the places, our God, where we met
       thee;
   Lest, our hearts drunk with the wine of the world, we forget
       thee;
   Shadowed beneath thy hand
   May we forever stand,
   True to our God, true to our native land.

© 1921, Edward B. Marks Music Company

The first stanza urges song—not, particularly, a song of praise, not even a song addressed to God. The song is to fill earth and heaven (line 2), to make them ring "with the harmonies of liberty." This suggests the *efficaciousness* of song, its transforming power. Harmony, after all, is a traditional metaphor for righteous order in creation, in which everything has its due place, "and God saw that it was good." The image of "the harmonies of liberty" is thus strong and powerful: our song has the power to fill earth and heaven with the righteous values of liberty. The ringing is both aural (a sound) and geometric. To "ring" earth and heaven is to encircle them.

The second set of three lines gives us "rejoicing" to parallel and explain that song, those harmonies. The rejoicing will be explained shortly, but we note how the activity is again moving *in space.* The ringing "earth and heaven" (both sound and circle) have been detailed to include the "list'ning skies." (The "list'ning skies" is a modestly theistic reference to some attentive deity.) That our rejoicing is to "resound loud as the rolling seas" is only useful from a perspective later in the song, when we come to the "way that with tears has been watered." For now it just sounds good; it resounds, rolling off the tongue.

The two long lines further explain this song as (1) "full of the faith that the dark past has taught us" and (2) "full of the hope that the present has brought us." As with the natural order and the listening skies, this faith and hope are not specific. We may well wonder *what* faith? *what* dark past? *what* hope? *what* present? These are not general Christian faith, history, present hope. They are, specifically, the faith of the African-American people, tried through the horrors of slavery, and the hope in liberation generated by freedom and the civil rights movement.

Confronted by the specificity of this text, white singers have two choices: One alternative is to *pretend,* while we sing this hymn, that our ancestors were victims rather than oppressors. I find this a morally questionable game, something like the Christian camp games my students have written about, in which the kids play at the experience of Christians-as-oppressed by evil powers. We may sing in solidarity with the African-American experience, meaning that "we really understand and sympathize with all you people have had to suffer" and want to help. But it seems to me that this does bad things to this text and all hymns as authentic expressions of our own spiritual condition. As a hymn, sung by white singers, this song becomes a game, however constructive, a chance to experiment with roles that are unfamiliar, even to which—as we value the Beatitudes—we are not entitled.

The second alternative is to make the text relevant, to read the experience it reflects as metaphorical. These particular sorrows of a particular people, this particular liberation from bondage, is analogous to general life sorrow and the bondage to sin and death we all share. We are thus all delivered, all called to sing in celebration and to dedicate our lives to righteousness. This reading is obviously problematic as it cancels the evident purpose of this hymn as an expression of solidarity, generalizing and unspecifying the central idea. It is further difficult because Johnson drew on the prototypical experience of the people of Israel and their deliverance. When we sing the hymn metaphorically, we return to that experience and, basically, ignore the experience of African Americans. We lose the point. (Just so, we may attempt to claim the text by injecting our own history of ancestors bound by poverty, confined to concentration camps, oppressed by sexism, but faithful nonetheless. This is no less reductive of this text as the particular expression of a particular historical experience in which we are all implicated.)

That Christianity is at best implicit in the first stanza comes clear in the last three lines. We might recognize the line "facing the rising sun" as the conventional pun (sun/Son). Christians, liberated from sin and death, "face the rising Son." But this text doesn't work that way: this is basically just a new day, more hopeful than the past but calling for continued marching toward victory. The image has more value as part of a configuration of light after dark than as a vision of the Resurrection. It is part of the pattern of nature—earth and heaven, skies and seas—that is being built up. The pun takes us nowhere.

The march toward *future* victory in the last line of the first stanza is continuous with the stony road of the *past* in the first line of the second stanza. The "chast'ning rod" recalls the violence of overseers. We *may not* separate this rejoicing from that past, by the terms of this text. That those were "days when hope unborn had died" hints back at the "rising sun," but it is stronger as an image of death. So stones, rods, stillbirth, weariness, and sighs convey the past, culminating in the *question* whether we have "come to the place for which our parents sighed." It's a good question: Is this freedom *it*, the goal?

As the second half of the stanza looks back over the "way," Exodus experience combines with African-American experience: "a way that with tears has been watered" combines the salt water of sorrow with the slaves' suffering through the Middle Passage. "The blood of the slaughtered" recalls the martyrdom of African-Americans, the slaughter of innocents, and perhaps death in the Red Sea. The stanza returns to light imagery at the end: the idea of emergence from the gloomy past, looking toward the future. (The "white gleam of our bright star" is very strange and obscurely astrological.)

In the third stanza we turn to address God, who has not been particularly in evidence until now. We can understand the perception that God has not been in evidence, given this experience of suffering. But the absence of God is not especially edifying. We find out, retrospectively, that God was there all the time, through the weary years. "God of our silent tears" is, for all its prettiness, obscure. It refuses to say anything about the relationship between God and "our" suffering—nothing about crying to God or God's comfort or vindication. That it refuses to help us cope is yet another indication that this song is, at best, very unconventional as a hymn. Hymns help us process such experience.

Rather, we go back to the "way," the path from past wretchedness to future victory, now understood as God's deliverance ("who hast brought us thus far on our way"). God has been present through history, active and somehow powerful ("by thy might"), leading us "into the light." This is, in the terms set up, simply the light of hope, of a new day.

"We" petition God to keep us in "the path," which may, metaphorically, be read as the path of righteousness, but seems more exactly the path toward victory, deliverance, leading to "the place for which our parents sighed." When we ask preservation from straying away and from worldly forgetfulness, we may think of lost sheep and holy places and biblical scenes of drunkenness—but the text is never insistent in these matters and leaves a lot of room for interpretation. The song never really asks for Christian commitment beyond dedication, under God, to the path toward liberty.

Indeed, this is the finale. That we are "shadowed beneath thy hand," given the light imagery, is a bit suspicious. The song has us *wanting* light (the "new day," "out from the gloomy past," "into the light"), so that the shadow of God's hand may make us wonder again about what God made of our silent tears. Actually, neither "True to our God" nor "true to our native land" is defined. What do they mean? I think we should get help here. The hymn has been telling "us" that we should be true to the path, the road, the vision. But then the relationship between God and our "truth" to God should be explored. The parallel expression is even more distressing, however, for all its resonance: truth to God and truth to our native land are on a level, compatible, seemingly easy. That's not consonant with the hymn's own message.

Experimental Hymnody

Not surprisingly, the two hymns presented under this heading share several features in common with our sample third-world and liberation hymns: These hymns, by Herbert Brokering and Jaroslav J. Vadja, are unconventional (in the narrow sense of the term), turning away from the tradition and going after new forms of song. The same general interest in alternatives has led editors to include third-world and liberation hymnody in contemporary hymnals. Experimental hymns all try to be "fun," catchy, to ingratiate singers in new ways. Their novelty *is* fun. They attempt simplicity, enjoy their own energy, and, while earnest, avoid the heavy burden of serious theological education. I think there's a covert political understanding here, too, an attempted resistance to elitism, an embracing of common values and experience and language and music. Folk song and popular song figure prominently, especially in the second example.

The critical task is supposed to be sympathetic. We are to read texts in the same spirit in which they were written. Accordingly, the standards of Watts's hymn pedagogy and precision don't belong here, and we shall try to examine these texts strictly in the terms of their own standards. Nevertheless, hymns—as congregational song, as poetry—cannot be allowed to renege on one basic requirement: to form our experience of faith.

Earth and All Stars

Herbert F. Brokering's (b. 1926) hymn "Earth and All Stars!" is certainly fun, a fitting place to start because of its urging us all to sing a *new* song. The hymn is basically very repetitive, with each stanza built on a psalm frame. When we let capital letters stand for who or what is enjoined to sing, we can roughly diagram the stanzas as follows:

Lines 1 and 2:	A, B, and C
Line 3:	Sing to the Lord a new song!
Lines 4 and 5:	D and E
Line 6:	Sing to the Lord a new song!
Refrain (7 and 8):	He has done marvelous things. I too will praise him with a new song!

Half of each stanza is thus repeated—we actually sing "Sing to the Lord a new song!" no less than twelve times in six stanzas. We note further that every line but one terminates with an exclamation point! This indicates a basic fragmentation of thought, line-by-line, and a profoundly "exclamatory" tendency. The fragmentation means that the text is basically a long list of things, enjoined to praise God along with the singer-as-me. This incantatory mode is reminiscent of "Alabaré," with the difference of the extraordinary, often puzzling, items and ideas urged to praise. With some cuts and modifications, Episcopalians, Catholics, and Presbyterians include the original Lutheran text in their hymnals:

Earth and All Stars

1. Earth and all stars!
    Loud rushing planets!
    Sing to the Lord a new song!
    Oh, victory!

Loud shouting army!
Sing to the Lord a new song!
He has done marvelous things.
I too will praise him with a new song!

2.   Hail, wind and rain!
Loud blowing snowstorm!
Sing to the Lord a new song!
Flowers and trees!
Loud rustling dry leaves!
Sing to the Lord a new song!
He has done marvelous things.
I too will praise him with a new song!

3.   Trumpet and pipes!
Loud clashing cymbals!
Sing to the Lord a new song!
Harp, lute, and lyre!
Loud humming cellos!
Sing to the Lord a new song!
He has done marvelous things.
I too will praise him with a new song!

4.   Engines and steel!
Loud pounding hammers!
Sing to the Lord a new song!
Limestone and beams,
Loud building workers!
Sing to the Lord a new song!
He has done marvelous things.
I too will praise him with a new song!

5.   Classrooms and labs!
Loud boiling test tubes!
Sing to the Lord a new song!

Athlete and band!
Loud cheering people!
Sing to the Lord a new song!
He has done marvelous things.
I too will praise him with a new song!

6.   Knowledge and truth!
Loud sounding wisdom!
Sing to the Lord a new song!
Daughter and son!
Loud praying members!
Sing to the Lord a new song!
He has done marvelous things.
I too will praise him with a new song!

© 1968, Augsburg Publishing House

I think it's safe to say that the human imagination naturally seeks pattern, progression, development. So we expect such a list to start somewhere and lead us somewhere. And indeed here we begin with what might be creation (heavenly stars and earth) and end with the worshiping community, all praising. In between, however, I have been unable to find any order at all. The items seem an anarchic rush, a heap of images, an arbitrary list. We are evidently not meant to dwell on any of these or to ask questions: whose victory and how can "victory" sing? any army? treacherous weather? Are all these things noise-producing, including the flowers? This isn't just "all that hath life and breath" but also dead leaves and abstractions (knowledge and truth). Musical instruments, suddenly, make sense, but then we wonder how limestone and beams and classrooms and labs sing. We skip around joyfully and arbitrarily. Anything goes and we mustn't stop the rush of enthusiasm to examine what we're saying.

The enthusiastic rush recalls Wesleyan hymnody and the joy of "Alabaré," but here it seems to have gone slightly mad. Wesley changed address often, but not *thirty-seven times*. What are we doing talking to all these objects and people and abstractions? The madness of disordered perception recalls Cowper's evil visions: "loud rushing planets" are certainly idiosyncratic, as is the singing limestone. The hymn verges on the surreal, on a cinematic phantasmagoria of rushing planets from *Star Wars,* boiling test tubes out of a mad scientist movie, singing laborers from a 1930s propaganda film, and cheerful crowds at a 1950s football game. Add a war movie (victory) and a pioneer flick (bad weather), mix with the psalm, and that's entertainment!

In fact we are back with our initial quest for an *understanding* of what praise is. This experimental hymn simply insists that we *do it.* The pleasure in repetition, simplicity, and novelty suggests that our quest for understanding is idle, beside the point. That seems to me to be a more considerable challenge to the tradition of intelligibility than any we have yet encountered.

This Touch of Love

Jaroslav Vajda's (b. 1919) communion hymn "This Touch of Love" is experimental because it uses the idiom and address of a popular love song and establishes a very private, personal, ecstatic mood. These approaches are unconventional—albeit related to the traditions of divine love and the exemplary "I." The sensual immediacy of the imagery—"experimental" in another sense—contrasts strikingly with less considered use of flashy, pop ideas.

This Touch of Love

1. This touch of love,
   this taste of peace,
   how can it last and still increase?
   I cannot bear
   to have this air
   of wonder cease.

2. This happy feast,
   this friendly bond,
   how can I keep it long beyond
   this fleeting hour,

this surge of power,
this treasure found?

3. This glow of joy,
   this glimpse of light,
   this momentary pure delight,
   I dread to leave
   to fret and grieve
   and die in night.

4. This freshly washed,
   this feeling free,
   I need to know that this can be;
   make me believe
   what I receive
   is meant for me.

5. Christ Jesus, you
   are what I need,
   the Bread and Wine on which I feed,
   no friend so true,
   no life so new—
   I'm rich indeed.

6. O Savior, now
   my spirit raise,
   give new direction to my ways,
   in all I view,
   in all I do,
   to give you praise.

© 1987, Jaroslav J. Vajda

The hymn demands reference to a sacramental context. It only makes
sense as part of a communion service, as a devotional process of reaction
to the sacrament. It nevertheless starts off as a pleasant secular love song,

contemplating immediate sensual joy, patterned as this touch, this taste, this air of wonder. "I" am amazed at the long surge of pleasure: this is the message of the question. The second half of the stanza counters the wondering question with anxiety, with distress, the anticipation of the end of the "high." The first stanza is vaguely disturbing as I think it's meant to be. In traditional mystical theology the sensual joy will end. Ecstatic experience raises questions.

The second stanza turns from intimate sensuality to an alternative pleasure. (The sacramental context remains a given.) Here the pleasure is social, a party of friends. But the anxious countermovement comes even earlier, in the second line. *I* want to sustain the pleasure but worry about the transient nature of such a high ("this fleeting hour"). Still, the singing self sees sustaining joy *as its own effort* and hasn't come to terms with what's going on. *I cannot* in the first stanza, and *how can I* in the second signal mistaken attitudes, however common, needing correction. Contrary to how we might normally think, this is not my doing, my achievement.

By the third stanza, the problem of transience, of the temporary nature of such a sensual or social sacramental high, has moved into first position in the first line. The threat to ecstasy has taken first place. A "glow," a "glimpse," "momentary pure delight"—these pass. Anxiety is foremost. The problem is the subjectivity of the experience. The grammatical form reflects the substance: the Lord has still not entered the picture. *I* am the agent and *I* dread to leave, to fret, to grieve, to die. "To die in night" recalls the sexuality of the love song with which we began, the end of the party of the second stanza, the shutting off of the light in the third.

With the fourth stanza we move to the second half of the hymn, which takes us in a more constructive direction, reprocessing the images and anxieties, and above all the self-absorption, of the first half. "This freshly washed" is baptismal, more exactly sacramental than any of the images in the first three stanzas. (It also suggests a good shower, which is perfectly fine.) "This feeling free," a parallel construction, is also rich in suggestion: the simple sensation of freedom, the idea of freed senses, freedom from sin and judgment—all combine.

The good sensations are, however, immediately challenged with a pressing demand: "I need to know." The sense experiences, the joys and fears of the subjective self, are, however lovely, insufficient. We want assurance, *to know* "that this can be." The simple "being" of pleasure, the pleasure of pleasure, however spiritual, is not enough. We need to understand, to know that this is intentional, purposive, has meaning, "is meant for me."

The third line, "make me believe," finally has the singer address God, asking for help, for faith. The faith begins with this turning to God and with this understanding that pleasures—physical, social, sacramental, however fleeting—are *gifts,* that is to say, "what I receive." The entire understanding of what's happening is being transformed, through the poetry, reflecting devotional progress. Having experienced (in the third stanza) the dread of death in the night, we have stopped asking questions and begun to pray.

This becomes explicit in the fifth stanza, clearly addressed to Christ. Christ as "what I need" answers all the *need* we have expressed for permanence and knowledge. Christ as "Bread and Wine on which I feed" recalls the taste and the feast of the first two stanzas. Christ as friend recalls the social pleasures of "the friendly bond." Christ as new life recalls the joyful moments of the third stanza and the shower of the fourth, all this while it cancels the death fear. "I'm rich indeed" transforms the "treasure found" back at the end of stanza 2. This is the realization for which the earlier stanzas were all a preparation, a path.

The realization cedes, in the final stanza, to a petition for the confirmation of this new orientation, this new faithful knowledge of what it's all about. "My spirit raise" asks for both a good, high-spirited mood, and for resurrection. It seems also to ask for a mystical elevation from the dark night of the soul. The second line, asking "new direction," is a new idea. Direction hasn't figured here, since we've been all involved in the self. (The idea seems to be that self-absorption is supposed to change.) In the language of the mystics, *direction* also implies spiritual direction and spiritual ways.

The endpoint, the goal, is praise. This is the point of our redirection, of the hymn as an organization of our sensations, as the proper orientation of its singers. To *give* praise recalls the new understanding of the gifts "I receive" as intentional, purposive, as "meant for me." Finally, we note how the pronoun *you* has been sung only twice. We worked toward it. In the fifth stanza, "I" acknowledged my *need* for "you." In the sixth, at the end,

"I" can respond to give "you" an offering of comprehensive praise.

Vajda's hymn demonstrates how very exciting experimental hymns can be. The text is novel in its colloquial expression, daring in its sensuality. But it coheres; it hangs together. It progresses, taking its singers from here to there. Singing it, we achieve something.

X: Modern Traditional Hymnody

The four modern selections that remain have all been published since 1961. They are all orthodox in their approach, in their understanding of what hymns do, of how they work. I have placed them under the "traditional" heading with the understanding that this is a compliment. It seems to me that the expectations and demands of the congregational hymn are so high and strong that a certain respect for the tradition is wise. (Vajda's text, treated in the last chapter, endorsed the point as it perhaps challenged our conservatism.) Of course, a good traditional hymn contributes something new as well, a freshness, a vigor, that makes the traditional seem modern.

A Stable Lamp Is Lighted

Richard Wilbur's (b. 1921) text "A Stable Lamp Is Lighted" is clearly the work of an accomplished poet. The art is evident in the clear images that come through the words, images much like photographs or paintings. We notice the old zoom-lens technique at work, surveying heaven and earth, from a distance and up close. The craft comes clear in the careful weaving of strands of meaning and the patterning of repetition and rhyme. The ideas are rich and complex, and we have to work a bit to make the hymn work. Words have multiple meanings, caught in networks of reference. The text is included in the Lutheran, Catholic, and Episcopal hymnals.*

The first two lines of the first stanza achieve several things. We move, first of all, from a "close-up" of the lamp to a "long shot" of the whole sky. This is an appropriate introduction to a hymn about a baby whose birth alters all creation. But more is happening here, an interesting grammatical item. In this hymn Wilbur has reserved the passive voice for the acts of God. This is ingenious as it suggests that no normal, active, subject-verb constructions are adequate to describe what God does. We pull back rather into passive acknowledgment of divine happenings. Then there are the multiple meanings: a "stable" lamp is both a lamp in a stable and a steady light—"stable" like the light of the world. Then there is the glow of the lamp, our close-up shot from a hundred Christmas cards, extending in wavelike arcs up and out and across the sky. It "wakes" the sky like a sunrise (the familiar sun/Son pun), although it's nighttime (hence the lamp). The arcs of light are also a "wake," like the wake that follows a boat on water, each wider and fuller. A "wake" also precedes a funeral, involving celebration and grief together. The glowing arc of light is also a halo, a radiant "glory."

In the third and fourth lines, heaven and earth are both drawn to worship. But Wilbur as poet resists the abstractions of "heaven" and "earth"

---

* The copyright holder's requirements, while appropriate for hymnal or music collections, were inconsistent with the budget limitations of a book such as this. Therefore, we are unable to provide the text for *A Stable Lamp Is Lighted.* The text can be found in *Lutheran Book of Worship,* 74; *Worship—Third Edition,* 385; and *The Hymnal 1982,* 104. We regret the inconvenience to the reader. —*Editor*

and gives us rather the stars and the stones. Stars with voices recall the music of the spheres, the harmony of creation. Their bending down their voices is a countermotion to the arching wake, reaching up. The Incarnation is being diagrammed as a physical phenomenon: the attraction of the baby's birth is a force that bends sound waves from outer space. The very stones that cry out represent the worship of the earth. The miracle of nature, of stars and stones, praising God is familiar from the Psalms.

The fourth and fifth lines of each stanza amount to a refrain set inside each stanza. This placement is, of course, unusual. It also calls for fine technical control. The clue to Wilbur's management is seen in the period separating the two lines repeating "And ev'ry stone shall cry." The line, deriving from Jesus' words "the very stones would cry out," means something slightly different in the fourth line, sung with reference to what goes before, and the fifth line, sung together with what follows. Stones, we may even conclude, don't cry with much variety, but the fact of their crying at all, taken in a larger context of meaning, is remarkable! So, in the first stanza, the crying stones in the fourth line represent earth, answering heaven (represented by the stars) as they worship the baby, the lamp of the world, lighted.

In the fifth line the crying of the stones goes together with the straw shining like gold, evidence of a transformed creation. Inanimate things, like stones and straw, become active, animated, renovated by the Incarnation. (Compare the singing limestone from the Brokering text, which might, with care, have worked like this.) The straw, shining like gold, takes us back to the stylized radiance of the Christmas card picture. (It may also recall the poor damsel who had, miraculously, to spin straw into gold in the fairy tale of Rumpelstiltskin. That association is just fine: the Virgin achieved no less.)

In lines 7 and 8 the idea of the barn "harboring" heaven pulls together the stable and the straw with the sky and the stars. *Barn* is a variant of *bairn*, an ancient word for "baby." More generally, barns, sometimes made of stone, "harbor" or protect straw, not heaven. Everything is changed. The idea of a harbor recalls the watery idea of the wake following the ship into harbor. To harbor is also to cherish or entertain, useful additional meanings in this context. The idea of barn as harbor is no less wild than the idea of a stall as a shrine. But that stall did become an actual shrine—witness the many centuries of faithful tourism in Bethlehem. Transformation is the order of the day.

In the second stanza we leap forward in time to Palm Sunday and Jesus' "triumph." We note again the agency of inanimate things called to worship, the praise of creation—"the palm shall strew its branches" and the stones that cry. Again, there's a subtle shift between lines 4 and 5. The stone first cries just as the palm strews—in homage now, not in adoration. Then, after the period, in the second half of the stanza, the stone's cry as miraculous is detailed. It is, after all, "heavy, dull, and dumb." Its heaviness, as an image of weight, may remind us of the bending voices of the stars, the attraction of the lowly. The dullness contrasts with the lamp, the glow, the shining gold. That something dumb can cry is simply extraordinary, as extraordinary as the incarnation we celebrate. That the stones have a function, paving the road to the Kingdom, is hopeful. The whole point, as we shall learn, is that "the low is lifted high."

The heaviness, dullness, and dumbness of stones are simple physical attributes of stones. They are also moral qualities of people as stones. They also contrast with the active, shining energy of worship. This multiplicity of significance is what we expect from good poetry. Meanings, all compatible, proliferate. Thus when these stones "lie within the roadway," they both simply sit there *and* cry out falsely, deceptively. Their Palm Sunday homage, like ours, is hypocritical—"lying" in another sense, as insincere. The same stone-people will cry for crucifixion.

The third stanza treats the Crucifixion as powerfully yet subtly as the birth. Again, God's activity is cast in the passive voice: "Yet he shall be forsaken" recalls Jesus' words on the Cross. *Yet* means both "nevertheless" (despite Palm Sunday) and the impending future (I haven't done it yet). That he shall be "yielded up to die" recalls the images of weight and effort. Those bending voices (the high bent *down*) and crying stones (the low raised *up*) find their object in the yielding *up* in death of Christ. Both the body raised onto the Cross and the "yielding up" of his spirit in death are such motions.

When the sky groans and darkens, the agony of Jesus is transferred to the sky. This is more than simply nature's response to something terrible.

Nature participates, all-involved, as it has from the beginning, when the glow of the lamp waked the sky and the stars bent down. Here the crying stones express themselves as part of this incarnation, all-involved. In the fifth line, finally we get what we've been expecting all along, the exact relationship of ourselves as people to those crying stones. It's worse than we thought: the stones cry out, aghast, at our human stoniness. We are worse than stones. Stones are naturally stony, albeit capable, through extraordinary redemption, of song. Our stony hearts, in contrast, are unnatural, less sympathetic than the very stones.

The last two lines of the third stanza give us a powerful zoom-lens close-up and an interpretation of it. The grammar of the stanza seems—appropriately—to break under the strain. "God's blood upon the spearhead" is, however brief, as violent as any Baroque Crucifixion tableau. Its economy forces home the bitterness of the message of "God's love refused again." Spearheads, like stones, are hard. Blood springs from the heart (our hearts, in contrast, are stony). It is, however, the word *refused* that draws our critical attention. Most simply, in crucifying Jesus, we rejected Jesus as God's love manifest. But in such a fine piece of poetry, where so much is going on, here at the climax of the hymn, the word *refuse* can't be skipped over! Let's try a number of possibilities:

1. *Refuse* is garbage, what we discard as unnecessary. Crucifying Jesus, we "trash" God's love again. This is stronger and more awful by far than simple rejection.

2. To *fuse* is, chemically to merge together. It may even mean having atoms in common. In this sense, "God's love refused again" means that in death as in birth, Jesus is one with us. The Crucifixion is the completion of the Incarnation.

3. A *fuse* is also "a detonating device for setting off the bursting charge of a projectile." In a hymn that begins with a lighting whose "glow shall wake the sky," we would certainly do well to watch for fuses. The bloodied spear is on a vertical axis, a projectile.

(The resisting reader may still wonder whether the poet intended all these meanings as he wrote the poem. That's a venerable and interesting question—which I, obviously, would answer yes—but it's not to our point here. The meanings are there and they fit together. They're not obscure or hard to come by if we simply slow down and explore the words on the page. They enrich our experience of the hymn as song, refining our devotional experience. They are worthwhile.)

In the final stanza we return to Christmas, the "now" of our song. The Christmas achievement is "as at the ending" in a number of senses. The stable lamp, whose glow woke the sky, was something "low . . . lifted high." It has been compared to the grown body of our Lord, "yielded up to die." The Crucifixion is "the ending." But of course, it's not the only ending. In the Resurrection, as well as at the Ascension and at the coming of the Kingdom, the low (dead) is lifted high. The whole process is initiated at the Incarnation, hence "now as at the ending."

"The low is lifted high" is cast in the passive voice—Wilbur's choice for the acts of God. It suggests weight raised, the effort of lifting, but most of all the reordering of nature, the exaltation of the humble, those valleys that shall be exalted. In this stanza, the bending voices of the stars and the crying out of the stones come clear as evidence of this reordering. Finally, in line 5, the stones cry in praise—as do we, despite our stony hearts.

The actual child is reserved for the end of the last stanza, a remarkable instance of restraint in a Christmas hymn. When he finally appears, we welcome him and understand, freed to praise. No simple divine visitation, his "descent among us" is part of a whole cosmic diagram of arcs and wakes and lamps and paving stones. Finally, cast in the passive voice, the reconciliation of the worlds comes clear as God's achievement. The "up" world and the "down" world are fused.

The hymn, as we have examined it here, is not easy. I have doubtless overlooked many items, particularly scriptural material. The difficulty is, however, not necessary. One may read the hymn and sing it much more simply as a series of images, of impressions, recalling Christmas cards and manger scenes. It's possible to take each line as it comes and not to look for patterns of larger meaning and reference. Possible, but not nearly so interesting or rewarding.

Rise, Shine, You People

If both Richard Wilbur's poetry and his devotional process bring the hymns of Watts to mind, Ronald Klug's (b. 1939) hymn of praise, "Rise, Shine, You People," sung by Lutherans and Methodists, recalls the better hymns of Charles Wesley:

Rise, Shine, You People

1. Rise, shine, you people! Christ has entered
   Our human story; God in him is centered.
   He [Christ] comes to us, by death and sin surrounded,
   With grace unbounded.

2. See how he sends the pow'rs of evil reeling;
   He [And] brings us freedom, light and life and healing.
   All men and women, who by guilt are driven,
   Now are forgiven.

3. Come, celebrate; your banners high unfurling,
   Your songs and prayers against the darkness hurling.
   To all the world go out and tell the story
   Of Jesus' glory.

4. Tell how the Father sent his Son to save us.
   Tell of the Son, who life and freedom gave us.
   Tell how the Spirit calls from ev'ry nation
   His new creation.

© 1974, Augsburg Publishing House

The opening command of "Rise, shine, you people" plays with a sergeant's order to the recruits to "rise and shine." That's good, but there's more. The sergeant giving a command probably doesn't think how the recruits are to rise and shine *like the sun.* He or she doubtless doesn't think of the sun as the Son who rose, or about rising and the Resurrection at all. Singing a Christian hymn, we do—or should. So the sergeant may mean "you people" (if those are even the words) as vaguely contemptuous. We sing as the "people of God," exhorting one another to proclamation as shining.

The substance of this proclamation is a dramatic event, a narrative, and its meaning. That is to say, "Christ the Lord has entered" or come into the room. We accordingly rise (perhaps remembering Wesley's lines, "Joyful, all you nations, rise"). That's appropriate behavior at the entrance of the Lord. But the line doesn't close with punctuation and the entrance is not simply *drama* (as in "Enter Christ, stage left"), it is also *narrative*. The Lord has entered "our human story." This shift in genre takes us by surprise, as well it should. We thought we were watching a parade and all of a sudden it's our story that is transformed. Our human story is both general and specific, both the story of the human race and your story and my story. Klug keeps after us to understand what's happening in all this exciting confusion, moving us from lordly entrance to story to diagram, yet another image. (These are all compatible, only the perspective shifts subtly. That God is "centered" in Christ the Lord is problematic, as it hardly seems Trinitarian, but the picture is good.)

The centering of God in Christ sets up a series of concentric circles. With the line "He comes to us," we return to the picture of Christ's progress. That we are "by death and sin surrounded" conveys the idea of our immediate circle of woe. As we sing, we tend inaccurately to attach the phrase to *He*, and to picture Christ as surrounded by death and sin in his coming to us. That's not bad or wrong, but it confuses our reading of the important last line of the stanza, where God's grace is "unbounded." That grace is "unbounded" in the sense of limitless or without bounds. As *we* are "bound" by the circle of sin and death, grace "unbinds" us, and we who were surrounded are now unbound. "Bounding" (as in leaps and bounds) also suggests the free energy of grace. (We might recall Neale's "strain" and "spring.")

The second stanza introduces its picture with the traditional injunction to "See" something. We begin with that diagram of centering when Christ the hero "sends the pow'rs of evil reeling." Here we have that centered energy, spinning away evil forces in an appropriately circular whorl. We next report his gifts, what he brings us. "Freedom" fits with the unbounding of the preceding stanza. Light and life are the counters to the death and sin that surrounded us.

The second pair of lines in this stanza steps back from the picture and suggests that our forgiveness alters our motive for action. "Forgiven," we are no longer "driven," hence presumably capable of a different kind of activity. The relationships between the bad things—the powers of evil (line 1) and our compulsion by guilt (line 3)—and the good things—freedom, light, life, healing (line 2) and forgiveness (line 4)—are not spelled out. (That's too bad.)

The opening of the third stanza recalls the first: "Come, celebrate" echoes "Rise, shine" as a command. Now, however, we understand more; our attention has been focused and we are specifically enjoined to *worship* and to *proclaim*. That we are to unfurl our metaphorical banners recalls that triumphal entrance at which we were to rise. "Unfurling" also belongs to the circular, whorling image pattern of centering, surrounding, bounding, and reeling. Hurling songs and prayers against the darkness recalls the opening command to shine, the death and sin around us, and Christ as light-bringer. The activity of hurling is energetic, even aggressive, a funny thing to do with songs and prayers. Indeed we generally sing and pray to the Lord rather than "against the darkness," but again, as with the centered God in Christ, Klug rescues and balances what might veer into heterodoxy.

Lines 3 and 4 of the third stanza exhort us to "tell the story / Of Jesus' glory," our other obligation, besides singing and praying. A "story of glory" is an active, heroic story. The heroics of the first three stanzas have led us to expect such, from dramatic procession to narrative self-awareness (of "our human story") to personifications of death and sin and powers of evil and banners and hurling prayers. This heroical understanding is certainly meant to recall German sixteenth- and seventeenth-century hymnody.

The last stanza gives us the substance of the story we are to tell, as well as a summary reworking of the hymn. That the "Father sent his Son" corrects any nagging misapprehension of God's centering in Christ. The saving action of the Son is a summary of all the things Christ was doing in the first two stanzas, amplified in the life and freedom of the second line. As we haven't been thinking about the Spirit (just as we may have been worrying about the Father), the last two lines are not anticipated and don't summarize anything. They may even seem to be taking us off in a new direction, to belong to another hymn. Their purpose is clearly to impose a suitably Trinitarian close. This is, of course, traditional, this doxological finale. Its awkwardness here suggests that perhaps the hymn isn't quite finished.

The energy and the striking images of "Rise, Shine" are exciting. The "voice," the singing self of the hymn is a vital, urgent call. We seem to be impersonating a leading member of the Christian community, urging fellow believers to action, understanding, energetic celebration, proclamation. "We" or "I" command "you people" to rise. This is "our" story and he comes to "us" and "brings us" freeing things. We are all forgiven, so we urge our fellow believers to unfurl their banners and hurl their songs and tell the story. This sounds a lot like the singer's role as preacher in many of Charles Wesley's hymns, a role that the sergeant's "rise and shine" introduced. The tradition indicates that this voice is as difficult to manage in a hymn as Christian ministry is in life, this combination of singer as individual leader, exhorting "you people," and at the same time, as representative believer.

Christ Is Alive! Let Christians Sing

At Brian Wren's (b. 1936) insistence, the text of his hymn "Christ Is Alive" is reproduced in its most recent (Presbyterian) version to the right side of the substantially different version sung by Lutherans, Catholics, and Methodists. (The Episcopalian last stanza is also noted.) The unfortunate consequence of Wren's contingent permission-to-print is that our reading of a widely popular text is compromised. We are drawn toward quite a peripheral interest, namely, the consideration of the personal history of a particular hymn writer's emerging sensibility. (This smacks of just the kind of personal-biographical hymnology we have forsworn.) Alternatively, we are encouraged to pore over the pedantic details of textual history—who wrote what when and who changed it. The work of a latter-day Martinus Scriblerus, the histories of the texts surveyed in this study would fill two hundred pages of footnotes.

Indeed, the complex history of such a young text raises interesting questions about hymns as *congregational* rather than *personal* poetry. Poets can certainly appreciate Wren's attachment to his latest draft. Scholars know that, in textual criticism, the latest version of a text is authoritative. If, however, the "old" (1968) version is sung by countless thousands of singers, are they misguided? Who is misguiding them? Which text matters, the one most people sing or the author's latest version? The authoritative, canonical status of denominational hymnals seems to be at stake. These are not anthologies of verse for singers to take or leave, but rather carefully reviewed and selected texts, approved for Christian worship. Are poets responsible? Are editors or review committees? If a text is flawed or confusing, whom can we hold accountable?

It would be lovely if Wren's latest version were a powerful improvement. Then hymnal publishers would eagerly issue a "hymnological recall notice" and distribute the new text for singers to paste into their hymnals. Unfortunately, the inclusive new version is only a modest improvement.

Christ Is Alive! Let Christians Sing

1. Christ is alive! Let Christians sing.
   His cross stands empty to the sky.
   Let streets and homes with praises ring.
   In death his love shall never die.

2. Christ is alive! No longer bound
   To distant years in Palestine,
   He comes to claim the here and now
   And conquer every place and time.

3. Not throned afar, remotely high,
   Untouched, unmoved by human pains
   But daily, in the midst of life,
   Our Savior with the Father reigns.

1. Christ is alive! Let Christians sing.
   The cross stands empty to the sky.
   Let streets and homes with praises ring
   Love, drowned in death, shall never
   die.

2. Christ is alive! No longer bound
   To distant years in Palestine,
   But saving, healing, here and now,
   And touching every place and time.

3. Not throned afar, remotely high,
   Untouched, unmoved by human pains,
   But daily, in the midst of life,
   Our Savior in the Godhead reigns.

4. In every insult, rift, and war
   Where color, scorn or wealth divide,
   He suffers still, and yet loves the more,
   And lives, though ever crucified.

4. In every insult, rift, and war
   Where color, scorn or wealth divide,
   Christ suffers still, yet loves the more,
   And lives, where even hope has died.

5. Christ is alive! Ascended Lord—
   He rules the world his Father made,
   Till, in the end, his love adored
   Shall be to all on earth displayed.

5. Christ is alive, and comes to bring
   good news to this, and every age,
   till earth and sky and ocean ring
   with joy, with justice, love and praise.

© 1975, Hope Publishing Company

Broken into no less than five sentences, the first stanza is severely fragmented. Each sentence sounds good initially but fails to connect logically to the others. Are Christians supposed to sing *that* Christ is alive? *because* Christ is alive? *that* "His cross stands empty"? If *empty* means devoid of content, is the Cross precisely "empty"? Even if Wren means that the body of Jesus is no longer hung on the Cross (which is doubtful, given stanza 4), is this really what we want to sing about? The body was removed, the Cross "emptied," for Jesus' burial. If we are celebrating that "Christ is alive," we had better sing about the *empty tomb,* rather than the empty Cross. Finally, why is the Cross empty "to the sky"? Although it suggests a simple picture of Cross and sky, I have been unable to figure out what the picture means. (I realize that I am taking on the traditional Christian language of the "empty cross" as emblematic of the theology of glory, and that this is a Christ the King hymn, but the words nevertheless need to make simple sense.)

We may presume that whatever exactly Christians are singing about, their song is the substance of the praises that are to ring in "streets and homes," a modernistic alternative to the echoes in the natural world, an alternative reminiscent of Brokering's noisy world of song. The picture is peculiar, however, to the extent that these would be very odd streets. Further, we note that the reason for praises, the subject of praises, the Lord whom we praise and his achievements—none of these items is indicated. Nor does the last line help: "In death his love shall never die." In *whose* death? the singer's or Jesus'? Or is this an abstraction, in death generally? Again, the declaration, however ringing, is imprecise and unrelated to what we've been singing about. We need to know if this is to make any sense. Is Wren saying something more than "Christ is alive" and "Jesus loves me"? These are fine, simple sentiments that don't demand such complex and confusing language. (The latest version of the last line, as it introduced a personified Love, drowning in some mysteriously liquid death but not dying, is wildly puzzling.)

Moving into the second stanza, perhaps searching for a solution to the puzzle, we announce again, perhaps trying again, that "Christ is alive!" Now we go on to declare that Christ is "No longer bound to distant years in Palestine." We may well wonder when and how and by whom he was thus bound. This is another crime—first drowning, now binding, headlined and then ignored. Presumably the Lord has always both acted in human history and transcended time. If we believe in the historical Jesus, then it is important that his life was "bound to distant years." That isn't a bad thing. By the same token, he has always come "to claim the here and now," and all of creation. Wren's formulations seem to make problems instead of clarifying them. (The new saving, healing, touching activities are politically correct alternatives to the militaristic claiming and conquering. "Touching" places and times, however, muddles a metaphor: people, objects, things may be touched. Places and times—as collective abstractions—are physically untouchable.)

The third stanza tries to explain that what we're trying to say is that Jesus is present, concerned, and that this is what we mean when we proclaim "Christ is alive!" The chosen metaphor is, unfortunately, Christ as King who reigns, and the stanza strives to justify this metaphor. The regal verb *reigns* works against this friendly Jesus, at least for people not ruled by a benevolent monarch who rules or reigns "daily, in the midst of life." Wren can only go at this through negative expressions: Christ is *not* "throned afar, remotely high, untouched, unmoved." We might well ask, Who said he was? The expression in a hymn of wrongheaded ideas or misapprehensions of God's relationship with humankind—even to correct or replace them—is questionable hymn pedagogy. We might well ask again, Why are we making trouble? Do people who think about Jesus tend to elevate him to a deistic position of "prime mover"? It's the first person of the Trinity who is treated like that in certain schools of philosophical theology.

It's just not a Jesus problem. (The new version, avoiding the "Father," leaves us with the very difficult idea of the Savior already *in* the midst of life, *in* the Godhead. Inclusive language needs to be clear and immediate. Such abstraction—even if it's used exactly—is ill-advised, particularly when the point would seem to be Christ's immediate, tangible, active presence here.)

The gist of the fourth stanza is the ongoing crucifixion of Christ through our sin. (The new version modifies this nice, traditional idea.) This is more coherent, this picture of how Christ "suffers still," but it is incompatible with the picture of Christ alive and the empty Cross. Wren, seeming to lose patience, simply settles for this paradox without trying to explain it. Redemption never enters the picture. Actually, it seems, we've skipped the Resurrection. We have a continually crucified, suffering Jesus and a living, loving present Jesus, but no salvation. The new, ghastly vision of a situation where "even hope has died" seems gratuitous.

The first version of the fifth stanza gives us the living Lord as ascended. We seem to have moved backward to the imagined problem of Christ "throned afar, remotely high" and the king metaphor. The pictures simply aren't fitting together. It begins to look as if Wren's objective was somehow to worry the idea of Christ the King, ascended and sitting at the right hand of God. We still haven't gotten very far, however, so we simply look to the future revelation when "his love adored / Shall be to all on earth displayed." This expression is virtual nonsense. First, there's the problem of the participle: "Love *adored*" by whom? Or does Wren mean, as the punctuation indicates, "his love adored shall be"? But that meaning runs into "to all" and won't work. And don't we deserve an explanation of this delayed display? The hymn has emphasized the obvious evidence of Christ's glory and love. Indeed, if there's any one cogent message here, it's the immediate omnipresence of Christ. How is it then that, although "His cross stands empty to the sky," the display of love will only come at the end? The hymn should tell us.

The Episcopalian version of stanza 5 provides yet another sort of violence: the consuming fire of the spirit, on into the future, when the meaning of it all will come clear.

5. Christ is alive! His spirit burns
   Through this and every future age,
   Till all creation lives and learns
   His joy, his justice, love, and praise.

© 1975, Hope Publishing Company

The latest (Presbyterian) version has Christ as messenger, now and whenever, until all creation is transformed. This seems yet another attempt to get to the point—but it's not the same point. The new fifth stanza might be a good launching pad for a complex new hymn, a hymn that will preach salvation or explain the transformation of nature (no longer streets and homes), or explicate joy, address justice, admit love, inspire praise. But that's a great deal to ask.

If Wilbur's hymn reminded us of Watts and Klug's hymn recalled Wesley, I would suggest that Wren's hymn betrays the difficulties of Cowper, whose work as a hymn writer was subverted by his own confusion. The Wren text also recalls how Grindal was tempted in her translation to leave the path of hymnody and wander through the bushes of theology. Only where obscurity can pass for holiness will such texts be sung as Christian hymns.

A Spendthrift Lover Is the Lord

"A Spendthrift Lover Is the Lord" by Thomas H. Troeger (b. 1945) was first published in 1986 in *New Hymns for the Lectionary to Glorify the Maker's Name* (New York: Oxford University Press). With its combination of tradition and modern appeal, the text, imperfect but very interesting, seems a fitting finale for our readings in modern hymnody.

A Spendthrift Lover Is the Lord

1. A spendthrift lover is the Lord
   Who never counts the cost
   Or asks if heaven can afford
   To woo a world that's lost.

Our lover tosses coins of gold
    Across the midnight skies
And stokes the sun against the cold
    To warm us when we rise.

2. Still more is spent in blood and tears
    To win the human heart,
To overcome the violent fears
    That drive the world apart.
Behold the bruised and thorn-crowned face
    Of one who bears our scars
And empties out the wealth of grace
    That's hinted by the stars.

3. How shall we love this heartstrong God
    Who gives us everything,
Whose ways to us are strange and odd,
    What can we give or bring?
Acceptance of the matchless gift
    Is gift enough to give.
The very act will shake and shift
    The way we love and live.

© 1985, Oxford University Press

The initial idea of the Lord as "spendthrift lover" dominates the first one and a half stanzas, preparing us for the "Behold," the spectacle of the second half of the second stanza. The last stanza defines our proper response. These items are immediately recognizable from the tradition as we have outlined it in these pages. The divine love metaphor, certainly, has been with us from the beginning. The injunctions to "See," "Behold," "Hark," and so on are routine, followed by appropriate response, modeled for each singer. The text nevertheless strikes us as fresh and modern, even daring. That's traditional too when we think back to the Baroque intention to startle singers into attention and realization.

If the Lord as lover is commonplace, the Lord as *spendthrift* lover is both extraordinary and strangely apt. We think of "spendthrift" as careless and improvident—a bizarre attribute for one who cares and provides for us. The most famous spendthrift, moreover, was the Prodigal Son, so that Jesus as prodigal son and lover comes to mind. This comparison works, however, as it forces home an idea of divine economics as totally other than, completely different from, human economics. That's a good idea, also grounded in the tradition. (Shakespeare's treatment of Christian generosity in *The Merchant of Venice* is a famous example.) The values behind sacrifice and salvation simply differ radically from those of thrift. We might still take exception to *spendthrift* because it doesn't exactly carry with it the idea of generosity. Our resistance is still economic, a natural repugnance to waste. We should resist the metaphor: that's how Baroque imagery gets to us.

The first stanza and a half will expand upon and detail this idea. That the spendthrift "never counts the cost" is simple enough, explaining *spendthrift*. *We,* not the Lord, wonder "if heaven can afford" this expensive venture. Cheapness and doubt as to heaven's solvency are, implicitly, *our* problem. *We* are, after all, accusing the Lord of being a spendthrift lover, a prodigal.

As he weaves together strands of loving and money imagery, Troeger carefully avoids the idea of the lover purchasing the beloved, an idea (however biblical) repugnant to modern sensibilities. Rather, the Lord *woos* "a world that's lost." That's love talk, suggesting desire and attraction, the Lord's drawing us to himself rather than compulsion. "The world *that's* lost" means two things at once. *That's* as a contraction means both "that is lost" and "that has lost." We *are,* of course, lost in sin and death. That we *have* lost suggests our poverty, our mistaken economy, redressed by the prodigal love of the Lord.

In the second half of the first stanza, the hymn enjoys as it explores the lover idea through two applications. The lover tossing golden coins across the skies is a sort of Mardi Gras parade picture, blown up to astronomical proportions. (The coins will be picked up and explained later.) The lover stoking the sun in the morning works similarly, combining the intimate bedroom scene with the solar system. Starry skies and warm fires belong to the world of love and wooing.

Divine love imagery is always violently restrained just as we're apt to get carried away. The second stanza, with its initial blood and tears, exercises the conventional restraint. The cost we've been singing about is blood and tears, not coins or firewood. That these are "spent" is appropriate: the word means both physical shedding and economic outlay. Just so "to win" both recalls "to woo," the lover's undertaking, and "to gain," or economic acquisition.

The third and fourth lines of stanza 2 indicate the major conceptual problem with this hymn, its fundamental confusion as to just who or what is the object of the spendthrift lover's wonderful attentions. Traditionally, the Divine Lover loves the individual soul. Divine love hymnody is thus basically an expression of very personal devotion. Troeger's love object is "the world." This works well as long as this world is "us" and the Lord is "our lover." It gets messy, however, when Troeger tries a social application, jumping the traditional track, as it were. The Lover's spending blood and tears to win the human heart collides metaphorically with the next two lines, about how this winning aims "To overcome the violent fears / That drive the world apart." These lines are unclear. What violent fears? We haven't been contemplating any such and they intrude unnaturally here. How do they drive the world apart and what does this activity have to do with the world as wooed, as coin-sprinkled, as sun-warmed? This isn't to say that another hymn on divine love and human distress couldn't be built around this idea. It's just to say that the idea isn't integrated here.

The latter half of stanza 2 commands our attention to the face of the lover, whose excessive spending has won us-the-world. Again, one finds the sixth line intrusive: that he is "one who bears our scars" has no function, no relationship to the pattern of ideas. Like the violent fears and divided world, the idea either belongs elsewhere or deserves considered integration. The seventh and eighth lines, however, are quite perfect. The spendthrift, indeed, "empties" his pockets just as Christ crucified is "emptied." The unimaginable "wealth of grace" draws all that economic language and love language into the understanding of the Crucifixion. This emptying of grace suggests a cup—of salvation, of blood, of the bitter cup not passing from Jesus. Those stars as coins of gold were signs of this spending.

The opening of the last stanza poses the question of response. God as "heartstrong" plays nicely on *headstrong,* like *spendthrift,* a near insult, suggesting our inability to appreciate God's love. The suggestion that his "ways to us are strange and odd," here at the end of the hymn, is, however, unsatisfying. Yet another near-insult, this one implies that we haven't gotten anywhere, that we've made no progress in the course of the hymn. If we have understood the ideas of the spendthrift, of generosity, of flamboyant and committed love, of the expense of blood and tears, of what's at stake; if we have come to appreciate God's "heartstrength," how can we still say that God's "ways to us are strange and odd"? That's a beginning point for a hymn, a puzzlement to be addressed.

The issue of offering, of response, is tricky here because of the central position of the economic metaphor for God's love. Our limited human understanding of generosity and prodigality has featured prominently. Troeger seems to have lost steam, to have forgotten all that he's been doing so well, and to opt for an idea of all this activity on God's part as simply a "matchless gift" and our "acceptance" of that gift as sufficient response. I suppose this is a version of the traditional offering as the gift of the self, of total dedication, but it's fairly weak. That our simple acceptance is an "act" that "will shake and shift / The way we love and live" leaves us puzzled. What does it mean to shake the way we love or to shift the way we live? The verbs *shake* and *shift* suggest rock dance movements or what shouldn't happen to fragile packages in transit, but hardly profound conversion.

This concluding imprecision may well belong to the larger pattern of problems and flaws identified above. In his drive to socialize the divine love analogy, the poet first gave us the world—as a collective of souls—rather than the individual soul as love object. Then, in stanza 2, he introduced those violent fears and the world as driven apart, again resisting the conventionally private vision of divine love without balancing its language or otherwise integrating the new ideas. In the questions of stanza 3 we observed Troeger's resistance to devotional progress, another convention. So, in the end, our response is a sort of new way of looking at love and life, more of a social readjustment than a profound transformation. The hymn does beautifully so long as it works toward our fresh understanding of a traditional idea. It gets into trouble by mixing hymn genres and expectations, by not understanding precisely the tradition to which it so nicely belongs.

Afterword

I offer a little afterword in lieu of a conclusion, hoping that I have supported the ideas I put forward in the introduction, defending the importance of hymns and their availability, as poems, for study. While I've expatiated on related subjects, my driving concern has always been this importance and this availability of these texts. While we have, in passing, observed patterns and traced conventions, the close readings of the thirty-six hymns rather than the patterns and conventions were the main point. While I have, as is only natural, tried to be convincing, these readings were never meant to be final and definitive interpretations. Criticism doesn't work that way. If they inspire protest, that's to the good. As it supports the importance of hymns and illustrates their availability for study, argument is right and proper. We haven't engaged in enough argument about hymns and what they mean. This is a discredit to our respect for words and for worship.

In part, I think the reluctance to analyze or to discuss what hymns mean is a result of the wonderful niceness of the Christian community. We want to be appreciative and affirmative and supportive—and criticism doesn't seem very nice, very kind. Hymns are written and sung in this close community of friends and relations. Hymns are, for the most part, amateur productions. We accept the offerings of friends and relations in the spirit in which they are offered. (The Christian community, like most families, argues regularly about politics and ethics, but rarely about words and imagery, sexual politics aside.)

The world of hymn writing and hymn translating and hymnal compilation is even smaller. We know each other, sit on committees and boards together, ask each other favors, pass each other jobs. (When I lead a workshop, a cousin or dear friend of the writer whose hymn I am discussing is apt to be in attendance.) In the spirit of collaboration we want to avoid criticism and correction.

This uncritical, affirmative attitude toward hymns—both in singing circles and in writing circles—has left us with some texts and translations that are virtually unintelligible, some that are misleading, others that have been badly cut and altered, others that would benefit from simple correction. We also have wonderful hymns, worth singing over and over, worth memorization and lifelong reflection. But we don't let them set the standard or lead the way. We won't discriminate.

Somewhere along the line we stopped reading carefully and completely. We stopped expecting language to matter. In my grimmer moods I think this just another sign of the decay of Western civilization—of education that doesn't insist that students understand, of a general intolerance of any communication that takes more than a few seconds. But then why do our creeds and prayers and Bible translations still make sense? People balk at incoherent sermons although they never wonder what "Hark! The Herald Angels Sing" is all about, words they sing and commit to memory. Nor can we blame the modern age when a text that is two hundred years old is so seriously flawed.

Sometimes I blame the immigrant experience, the generation of German and Scandinavian children who, having learned hymns in a language they didn't really understand anymore, the language of their parents or grandparents, never expected much from hymns. Or I blame the immigrant pastors whose English was shaky and didn't expect English to bear the strain of Old World poetry. But that doesn't explain the weaker items in the Episcopal, Methodist, Presbyterian, or Catholic hymnals or the flaws of contemporary British hymns or even the hollowness of Heber.

Sometimes I blame musicians—my good friends—who have, within my own memory, so speeded up hymn singing! The eye and mind need time to make sense of words. Or I blame the editors who break up the verses to arrange them between lines of music. When hymns don't look like poems, we don't expect succinct meaning.

After all is said, blame isn't in order. What we need is a recommitment to the intelligibility of hymns. We must hold these texts accountable as communications. In a loving family the letters we send each other are read carefully. We are alert for hints of unhappiness or other subtle signals. The same respect should be accorded our hymns. The result should be a new appreciation of all these texts can do for us, teaching and directing us, refining our devotion.

The intelligibility of hymns is especially important as we wake to a new day of evangelical outreach to unchurched people—white or people of color, native speakers of English or those who struggle with the language. We might expect our children—as perhaps we were expected—to continue the tradition of mindless, ritual mouthing of hymn words. It's wrong to expect this uncritical attitude from visitors to our churches or from new Christians.